ALSO BY THE AUTHOR

THE PLUS

SELF-HELP FOR PEOPLE WHO HATE SELF-HELP

GREG GUTFELD

Threshold Editions

NEW YORK   LONDON   TORONTO   SYDNEY   NEW DELHI

To Elena Moussa
(some lady I know)

Threshold Editions
An Imprint of Simon & Schuster, Inc.
1230 Avenue of the Americas
New York, NY 10020

First Threshold Editions hardcover edition July 2020

THRESHOLD EDITIONS and colophon are trademarks of Simon & Schuster, Inc.

For information about special discounts for bulk purchases, please contact Simon & Schuster Special Sales at 1-866-506-1949 or business@simonandschuster.com.

The Simon & Schuster Speakers Bureau can bring authors to your live event. For more information, or to book an event, contact the Simon & Schuster Speakers Bureau at 1-866-248-3049 or visit our website at www.simonspeakers.com.

Interior design by Jaime Putorti

Manufactured in the United States of America

1 3 5 7 9 10 8 6 4 2

Library of Congress Cataloging-in-Publication Data
Names: Gutfeld, Greg, author.
Title: The plus : self help for people who hate self help / Greg Gutfeld.
Description: First Threshold Editions hardcover edition. | New York : Threshold Editions, 2020. | Summary: "From *New York Times* bestselling author Greg Gutfeld comes a self-help book for those who don't believe in self-help, advising readers with his trademark humor and skepticism how to command ourselves to make positive decisions"—Provided by publisher.
Identifiers: LCCN 2020008528 (print) | LCCN 2020008529 (ebook) | ISBN 9781982149918 (hardcover) | ISBN 9781982149925 (trade paperback) | ISBN 9781982149932 (ebook)
Subjects: LCSH: Self-actualization (Psychology) | Decision making.
Classification: LCC BF637.S4 G89 2020 (print) | LCC BF637.S4 (ebook) | DDC 158.1—dc23
LC record available at https://lccn.loc.gov/2020008528
LC ebook record available at https://lccn.loc.gov/2020008529

ISBN 978-1-9821-4991-8
ISBN 978-1-9821-4993-2 (ebook)

CONTENTS

CONTENTS

THE PLUS AND THE PANDEMIC

I pretty much finished this book on the second week of January, 2020.

Around the same time, I was reading about some weird sickness erupting in China.

Tipped off in a Periscope podcast by Scott Adams, I started to obsessively pay attention to the frightening videos of nurses weeping in hospital scrubs, as body bags piled up.

Roughly ten days or so later, I went on *The Five* to demand we shut down travel from China to the United States. It should have been said sooner, but the media was still yakking about impeachment. Yep, impeachment–the predetermined failure that occupied the press and their accomplices in government.

Imagine, if just one reporter peeled himself away from that bitter exercise in futility to see what was going on in Wuhan, who knows if things would have been different. (A few of them, at Fox, did, actually.) Instead this idiotic adventure gobbled up the breathless media, the government, and the president. Sorry . . . I know that assigning blame is pointless right now. *It's a minus. Let's be a plus.*

I sent the book off, and that seems like another century ago. Since then we've experienced a once-in-a-lifetime event that has changed our lives. We shut down our economy, watched the stock market crash, and socially distanced ourselves, as storefronts closed and odd people hoarded toilet paper. Also, people died. But hopefully, far, far fewer than expected, because of our collective action. Oh, how I hate that word "collective." It's always on a flyer pinned to a bulletin board at an independent bookstore ("Come join our vegan pacifist collective poetry group meeting every third Thursday of every month unless Mercury is in retrograde or I overslept"). It's usually a code word for "angry weirdos with purple hair."

But in this case, this "collective" was 340 million strong, and we're, I hope, getting it done.

You could say "This is just like a movie." But it's not. Because in a movie, America would descend into violent chaos. Our streets would fill with maniacs. We'd turn on each other.

Reality, so far, proves the movies wrong. We didn't turn on each other. We turned *toward* each other. Obviously from a distance. But we did so to kick the virus's ass. I can't say if we've kicked its ass yet, because it's the middle of April, and I am in lockdown, like you. But I'm cautiously optimistic. Or optimistically cautious.

Because regardless of risk of sickness, and even risk of death, people are running toward the crisis—not away. How did we do that?

First, we accepted the brunt of the sacrifice, as a country. We voluntarily accepted draconian limits on our freedoms. We did it to save others, not just ourselves. Many of us could have continued to live normal lives. Most Americans under sixty-five probably would have been fine. In a country of 340 million, 1.5 million dead—that's a third of 1 percent. Nearly 3 million die each year anyway, from all sorts of stuff. Who cares?

Well, we did. And we still do.

We refuse to stomach that loss. We could have let this virus run its course, but instead we dramatically changed our lives, to save those lives.

Sure, some went on spring break, but since when is it news that young people do stupid things? I just wish their parents hadn't paid for their flights. They're the jerks in this story—because they're adults, with actual brains.

Let that go. After all, so many people did so many great things.

There are the doctors, nurses, paramedics, ER staff, and rest-home workers on the front lines, doing what was necessary, even if it might kill them. Ranchers, farmers, and truckers keep the food going, grocery clerks restock as they deal with panicked customers and hoarders. Pharmaceutical companies donate meds. People float loans to workers. Every person who could offer some benefit has done so. In this crisis, it's like assholes simply disappeared (although you could still find a few in the media, in the usual spots).

Everyone became a plus. Which made it harder for the minuses to hide.

As my wife could attest, I have almost no real talents that could save the earth. I can't fix things; I only break them. I am not the person to ask when you need help moving.

However, the help I give—if you ask—comes in a check. I'll pay for the move, so we can go out and drink.

That's one of my two pluses. I throw cash at people's problems. The other plus: offering optimism and hope on the shows I host. I think that matters.

It's a strange coincidence that I decided to write a self-help book about becoming a better person, before a massive, horrifying event that demands all of us to become better people.

I can actually put the principles into action myself. And I can watch others do the same. It's unreal, how the chapters seem to fit with this challenge.

For example, in this book I suggested cultivating your own curriculum–learning new skills to make you feel extra awesome. And, lo and behold, that has become a potent prescription during the claustrophobic moments of this pandemic: if you're home right now, and can't do anything—I say that you can: consider this moment an opportunity to get better at stuff (and life). I say this, though, realizing it's not so easy when nothing's going into your bank account.

So I focus on my health—or rather, my belly—which is easy to focus on, because it's right there in front of me like an evil Siamese twin made of butter and alcohol. I use the time to get in shape. And it's not hard. I don't push myself. I just walk. Or I ride. I'm not winning any medals in anything other than modest self-improvement and declining body odor. I also spend idle moments playing guitar and writing absurd songs about the pandemic—songs that you will never hear because they're worse than the virus.

The days grow longer, but I fill them with positives. I get up early—and instead of listening to the news (which does little for my mental health), I go for an hourlong walk, outside, alone. It gets me out of my brain and feeds me vital vitamin D direct from the sun. Then I hit the bike, indoors. My gym is closed, and I don't want to use that as an excuse to turn into a housebound flab mountain (ultimately, a crane will have to remove me through a hole in the roof).

The point is, there has never been a better time to become a better you than now. To turn your minuses into pluses. And this is happening after I wrote a book on how to do that.

If I'm not Nostradamus, then neither is he.

Then there's my "prison of two ideas" theory, in which we cling to a misguided belief that only two opposite positions exist on an issue, leading us into a constant dead-end face-off, when in fact there's an infinite number of stances existing between two oppositional beliefs. It's basically throwing two straw men into a ring and instructing them to fight to the death. They both lose.

Here's a "prison of two ideas" example that hinders our fight against a virus: Do we fight the pandemic, or do we save the economy?

That two-idea prison means that you can't do both at the same time. Yes, you can fight the virus and protect the economy, in phases, or at the same time. Which I hope you will see soon, if you haven't seen it already (again, this sentence is written on April 12, 2020).

This prison of two ideas is especially deadly because it

forbids you to ask the important questions–like when to re-open an economy! That's not a heartless question when you're talking about 340 million souls. You gotta think of the consequences not just of disease but hopelessness.

The fact is, we need to fight the virus through social distancing, which hurts the economy. But once we slow the spread ("flatten the curve"), we can reignite parts of the economy by phasing work back—either through age groups, health status, region, or a combination of such factors.

If you eliminate the two-idea prison, you find that you can toggle between two goals to find the best recipe that can save both lives and an economy. It might be that people over sixty stay home longer; and people under forty get back to work sooner. Our response to this pandemic proves that the two-idea prison is an obstacle to real solutions. It's never "either/or"—it's actually "this and that." There's an infinite number of choices between "total shutdown," and "We're 100 percent open for business." Smart people (you and me) understand this flexibility. The media, sadly, doesn't. Flexibility also allows us to pull back and change course if the virus decides to return (it will).

I could go on and on about the weirdness of this book's coming out now. I didn't expect this pandemic and neither did you. I just woke up in the middle of the night six or seven months ago, thinking about a book that might matter one day, maybe after I am gone. I didn't expect it to matter this much, this soon—but now I think it does. I am not patting myself on the back (my arms are too short). I am just grateful that maybe this pile of words will help you through tough times and turn you into a plus, when the best version of you is so desperately needed. What's weird: some of the chief complaints in this book will have been vanished by the virus. It's as if cancel culture and identity obsession took a rain check as real shit hit the fan, and unity told that other crap to scram.

One thing that cannot be overlooked is how the losses we are incurring are losses we experience together. No one is gaining an edge; we are all pretty much in the same place together.

I have no doubt that during this time you are answering the call of your family, your friends, and your country. You instinctively know what it takes to pitch in, to be a plus.

And once you understand that, there's no going back.

THE PLUS: THE ROAD TO RECOVERY IS PAVED WITH REASONABLENESS

When the going gets rough, good people lighten up.

One purpose of the Plus is to create an environment of reasonableness. Meaning that rhetoric in any bad situation should lean away from the intense and emotional, and toward the light-hearted and helpful. This is how you avoid being a minus, and instead become a plus, in a pandemic. And in life in general.

Ignore the divisive, and punish with memes

During the lockdown, New York City mayor Bill Deblasio produced a video in which he demanded citizens narc on other citizens if they violated quarantine restrictions. This, after he had earlier dismissed the hazardous nature of the illness. This was his way of making up for lost time: turning the public into the secret police. How fitting that after this stupid act he gets caught, on video, violating his own quarantine! He is truly a minus: For in a time of great strife, he chose to pursue a behavior that would divide us by asking that we turn on—and in—each other.

Who was the plus? All the Americans who left insulting memes and other nonsense on de Blasio's tip line. Yep, instead of reporting on each other, our country's patriots clogged his tattle-tale tip line with garbage. That is not just a plus—it's a patriotic plus. Instead of indulging in the very worst behavior in a time that screams for unity—narcing on each other—Americans chose instead to ridicule and annoy the offending culprit. Let that be a model for all of us.

Keep the briefs in the drawer

Let's say your neighborhood bar reopens. What do you do? Well, if you're a plus, you pay it a visit and spend some of your money to help him out. If you're a minus, you sue him for inadequate hand sanitizer in the restroom.

See, we need to allow civilization sufficient time to restart before we let the lawyers wake up and get to work. Because once a lawyer is in the room, nothing gets done until ten years from now. Seriously, would any of the great inventions have occurred if lawyers were in the vicinity of said inventions? Do you think we'd have electricity? No, Ben Franklin's kite would have been impounded as a public hazard. Do you think we'd even have fire? Of course not. It's hot! And you can't put a warning label on it! So, for now, in order to be a plus, let's slow-walk our legal actions and let society get back on its feet. Then, when we're back to 100 percent, we can sue the pants off each other (as long as we leave the masks on).

Put your finger away

Just about every single person on earth made incorrect predictions about the virus. The exceptions who didn't, didn't make any suggestions or predictions at all. They would never commit. If you said "If we don't reopen soon, our economy will implode," this fence-sitter might say "Yes, but we don't want to open too early!"; then, if you said "I worry that the disease might return," he might say "But you can't keep closed forever!" He's the never-wrong armchair quarterbacking gawker—never offering anything beyond banal platitudes designed to cover his butt. So later, without actually ever presenting an actual thought that carried a risk, he can show up to question timing, phasing, and so on—without ever having any real skin in the game. Which is why, here, I must reintroduce Gutfeld's law, which goes like this: "If you contributed nothing at the time of the event, then you can't point fingers in the future." Meaning that if you're one of those jackasses who like to pretend they predicted the outcomes only after the outcome presented itself, you deserve no attention from any of us who actually grappled with the tough adult questions. So put your blame-pointing finger away and stop wasting our time. We're trying to be a plus here; and your finger is just a big minus—a weathervane that tells you only how the wind blew a month ago.

INTRODUCTION

WHY I'M MAKING THE MISTAKE OF WRITING A SELF-HELP BOOK

One afternoon, on *The Five*, in the middle of yet another gripping segment about polarization, I said something about how I'd handle dealing with disagreeable people in this so-called age of division.

I won't tell you what I said, because then this book would be over. And you'd put this back on the shelf, without purchasing it. And I would be a little poorer, and a little more distant from my dream of owning a mattress castle (it's a castle made of mattresses; I think there's only one, and it's in Finland).

But when I got home and checked my email, I found one million strangers who watched the show telling me how much it meant to them (actually, it was thirteen). Some included their phone numbers. Secretly, however, I knew what I said would have some power. I had mentioned it on *The Five* to see if it would stick.

But like I said, if I told you what it is here, on page 2, then you wouldn't read the rest of this short little book (and don't skip to the next chapters, you cheapskates). So, I'm going to lie to you and say the answer to all our problems was coconut water enemas—just so we can move on.

So it came to me that my next book—that is, this one— would be one containing advice about solving the crap that's destroying all of us.

Horror of horrors, I would write a self-help book.

I felt gross, all over. Why? Well, I don't like self-help books because I don't like the people who write them. I know for a fact that the writers who give advice are generally severely screwed-up people.

Because I was one of them.

Yep, in a previous life, before you got to know me on various shows on Fox News, I was a writer and editor for mass-market service magazines. I began at *Prevention* magazine, once the largest health magazine in the world, starting as an assistant editor, soon to become their fitness editor. I wrote columns called "Interior Body-Building" and gave advice on nutrition and stress to scores of middle-aged women. I was doing all of this while eating steaks every night, drinking my weight in wine, and suffering panic attacks on stair-climbers. But dammit, I was so good at giving advice that they kept promoting me, until I became editor of the world's largest health magazine for men, *Men's Health*. (If you don't remember it, imagine a half-naked guy on the cover with abs that resemble a flattened accordion. That was essentially every issue, give or take an ab. That was twenty years ago, so those guys on the cover are likely now doing erectile dysfunction commercials.)

It was there that I lived the life that rejected all sound advice, as I told people how to live. Those who can't do, etc. . . . I thought I'd never return to that life, but alas here I am, giving advice once again. Why?

Good question. Let me think.

Okay—I'm doing this book, because I had a lot of ideas and a lot of diagnosed problems about the world in general. And frankly, I was sick of hearing about them, from me. If you think I can really annoy the crap out of people, imagine what I do to me. I cannot ever get away from me. I am stuck with me. And it can be as bad as you think.

Yep, I had too many brilliant ideas for books, and every day, each one triggered a major problem or challenge. I wrote many proposals, all of which were accepted by my wonderful publisher and editor, until I felt more than ready to go. I'd already figured out what to spend the advance on (creating an amusement park for people of my height). I would deliver a book or two that examined these persistent societal problems, and like my previous ones, sell enough to pay for all the surgeries designed to make me look more like a Shetland pony. Eventually, I noticed a glaring problem with all my ideas: they identified problems, but they were short on solutions. I was cranking out crap; I was feeling like a crank. Full of crap.

That was when I called my publisher in frustration and told them that while I could write the next book (it was halfway done), I felt like I was sleep-writing—performing a perfunctory duty on autopilot, which, believe it or not, works better with relationships than it does with writing. The book read fine as is, and it had some jokes and surprising wisdom, as well as the usual sparkling insight you'd find in my previous books . . . which also was the problem. I felt like I had done this before. I started to wonder if I was getting in a groove, or stuck in a rut, or caught in a trap while weasels ripped my flesh. I got sick of my own voice, saying the same old stuff. I wanted a new conversation with my readers; we'd exhausted the old one. I'm not coming down a mountain with scrolls—I just want to take the next step.

And then it came over me like a wheelbarrow of lumpy haggis.

Why not . . . *not* do it? Why not do something else?

I toyed with fiction.

I started writing a novel but realized I was a pretty crappy fiction writer. I didn't believe "me" because I was writing about something that didn't happen. I could feel myself making stuff up, getting deeper into the lie, until I just couldn't take it seriously. I asked for advice from various successful fiction writers, and they told me to write it as if it were real—as though I were reporting it. (They also told me other things, which I think they found witty but I, frankly, found insulting.) I tried that too—but every time I tried to write a new character, I felt like a big fat phony. So I gave up.

So you may ask why I am doing a self-help book, now.

Perhaps it's punishment (mine, not yours).

Or maybe I realize that now, roughly twenty years later, I actually know stuff about the world that should be passed on. You know you're getting old when your age matches a highway speed limit. So now, as I write this at fifty-five, I find myself in the happiest moment of my life. And I feel like I'm getting happier. This could be directly related to aging: Jonathan Rauch wrote a great book on this, one I interviewed him about, called *The Happiness Curve*. In it he detailed how, as you age, things don't get worse—they only get better (provided you don't die). I totally agreed with the premise, although I might have laughed at it when I was twenty-five. But I was young and dumb back then—now I'm old and smart (and insulated with muscular fat composed of equal parts creatine and McRibs). You've heard the phrase "I wish I knew then what I know now." Well, that's impossible, because in order to know what you know now, you have to leave the "then," far, far behind. Sorry: Being young isn't worth the trouble. The sooner you get old, the better.

If you aren't getting happier as you're getting older, you're doing it wrong. Either that, or you had the greatest childhood ever—which is sad, in a way.

So, now, as an old guy, I am equipped and able to write a self-help book that is meant to help you as much as it helps me.

This book is based on an epiphany born from a desire. The desire was to seek a solution to problems instead of merely cataloging them, and the epiphany was a simple system that is so easy to operate even a twenty-five-year-old "me" could do it in his underpants, provided I owned a pair. And it made writing a book about it so easy I could do it with one arm tied behind my back, because I only use one finger to type.

In these next chapters, I will go through the current, most relevant problems our country is facing—each of which ended up almost becoming a book in and of itself, except they lacked solutions. Which is why the voice in my head said I needed to stuff a sock in it until I find the solutions. Which I did.

So what follows will be a brutal unfolding of some very troubling issues we're dealing with right now. Mind you: these are psychological problems that can destroy you. The good news: because they're rooted in psychology, they might be the product of my own disturbed thinking. Which means you can beat them—since they're more my problem than yours!

My diagnosis of this problem leads to the solution. You have it in your hand.

It's "the Plus."

It's not about the power of positive thinking. It's about—without sounding positively nauseating—positive *being*. Every choice is a coin flip: plus or minus? Command yourself every morning to choose a positive path and avoid or eliminate anything that can be seen as a minus.

So it's not "random acts of kindness," or "paying it forward," or "thinking positively."

All of those are temporary, feel-good dalliances that require almost no discipline.

My thing is permanent, and irreversible. It's actually brainwashing, if it works correctly.

And yes, that sounds a bit "culty"—I'm okay with that.

Usually when you accuse anyone of pushing some cure-all, like a cultist attempting to brainwash the naïve, they'll deny it. Not me. I want this to brainwash the naïve. I want it to be a cult. I'd like it go grow beyond a cult—to reach the importance of say, a Maroon 5 fan club, or an organization that swims naked in the winter. If it reaches Scientology proportions, I'm totally okay with that; at least I might get a boat out of it. Or a nude swim.

The entire premise of my solution for all the problems I mention in this book boils down to one sentence you should ask yourself every morning. Over time, that query will be something you instinctively ask yourself before every meeting, every phone call, every date, and every dinner. But it begins tomorrow morning when you get up and face yourself in that bathroom mirror. That's when you ask yourself: "Will I be a plus, or a minus?"

The simplicity of such a question holds real power. We know the direction of both symbols—a plus means adding something positive to life; a minus means taking something away.

It's a polarity, but between them are an endless array of opportunities for good things and bad. Choose right at every time and you'll be able to beat the hell out of Dale Carnegie (which I once did, actually. It was easy, though—he was in his eighties and I had an axe).

I started this as an experiment several months ago. By nature, I am a cynical person, maybe not godless, but allegedly agnostic. I had spent a lot of time around angry people, and I myself am often mistaken for angry when in fact I'm just loud. I am not sure how it came to me, but in the middle of the night, tired but sleepless, exhausted but incapable of slumber, I realized that I was tired of running through my complaints over and over again. I realized that the roads I habitually traveled were not going anywhere new. I was on a daily commute to nowhere. I wondered if it was because I was choosing roads that only offered a tour of the problems, without taking me to a solution.

That morning for some reason, I said to myself—will I be a plus or a minus?

As an experiment, I said "Okay, plus." And I had that inside my head when I became faced with any decision that came my way.

If someone sent me an email that irritated me, I asked myself before I responded: Am I going to be a plus or a minus? And is my current mood influencing how my response might turn out? This is the key to everything in life: almost all my negative responses are mood based. And moods change as frequently as the underwear at incontinence camp.

When I read something defaming me on Twitter, before I responded, I asked myself: Am I a plus or a minus? And while I'm pondering this, I asked myself, have I been drinking? And if not, why not? This is the kind of thinking that drives me to the gym, where the pluses come in reps and resistance. But asking that question steers me into directions of least harm.

I made this self-quiz a routine for a few days. I felt that I had to say the actual phrase, out loud, to direct me toward a path of positive outcome. I'm pretty sure it worked. I feel like I eliminated a lot of stress, a lot of wasted energy, and more quickly forgot the things that used to regularly bother me. Deciding to be a plus, is perhaps, willfully embracing amnesia. I was forgetting what had just happened, what I had just seen on TV, and decided to give life a chance after the next commercial break.

I was also forgetting the things I had gotten used to. Part of life's negativity is born from boredom and predictability. It's one thing I learned from being around comedian Tom

Shillue, a religious and intense man who finds a Catholic church in every town we're about to perform in (we tour together). He is habitually surprised by life. I swear if I showed him the same Snickers bar he had seen minutes earlier, he'd react with glee and light a candle. Part of his robust mental health, I realized from traveling with him, is his outlook. He literally "looks out." (It's not called an "inlook" for a reason.) And everything that makes me nervous, he revises verbally, to me, as an adventure.

I'll say, "Tom, it says here that the venue is three hours away and the weather is terrible." He'll respond, "Imagine what could happen, Greg!"—as if that's a plus not a minus. He literally reverses that single catastrophic thought in my head into an exciting trip to an amusement park called life. He replaces dread with curiosity. It works.

A friend of mine with three daughters used to tell me about the sharp, painful Barbie accessories—tiny purses, brushes, and heels—that littered his living room carpet because his girls owned 1.5 million Barbie dolls. When he'd take his family to Walmart, the three happy children would immediately disappear into the Barbie aisle—and emerge heartbroken because all they could find there were the two Barbie dolls they didn't already own, and one was Ken. They needed plus-therapy. I suppose that part of being a plus is clearing the mental slate, so old things are always new. And you suddenly appreciate all the stuff you've already had.

The biggest minus in our lives is the desire for novelty: it drives us to hurt the people we already love and who already love us back, and to do dumb things with dumber people who love us only for the novelty they're getting from us, too. The desire for novelty fueled problems of the past, but because we have so many easier ways to cater to our thirst for "the strange," it's gotten worse. Take pornography—all it is is a product designed to satisfy the need for sexual novelty. But when I was a teen, you had to really work hard to get the stuff (most porn in the 1970s was hidden in hedges at the park, left behind by other older kids who couldn't let their snooping mom find it). Now every laptop is a porno-faucet; you can see everything and anything to satisfy your biological thirst for novelty. If I go to Pornhub and type in "lesbian Italian African babysitter mechanic gray hair speaks minimal Mandarin, owns a flute"—I'll get a dozen options (and one video I starred in under my stage name, Rock Logsworth).

I'm pretty sure that can't be good in the long run, but what do I know? One could easily counterargue that with the rise of accessible pornography came a decline in sexual assault. It's weird how statistics undermine your concerns. Example: as distrust over government continues to grow, so does the size of its budget. Weird, huh?

Novelty drives everything from pornography to painkillers—but what made us discover new countries could now be destroying our own. Which is why, when faced with a decision that risks the joys you already have, saying yes is always going to be a minus. Walking away is the plus.

So, over time, asking myself whether I was a plus or a minus became so routine that it no longer required saying it. It just happened to float above me, like an ice cream cone on my forehead, as I made my way through a typical day. Sometimes, true, I'd lose my cool, or I'd do something unnecessarily cruel. But according to my HR spy, I soon reduced those instances by two-thirds. I went on a cruelty-free diet the way people go on carb-free diets. It works, even with one cheat day.

In the next pages I will briskly touch on other major obstacles to living a happy, productive life in this particular day and age—and counter each with some plus-size solutions. Whether it's our self-destructive social media, the contentious world of actual personal interaction, or how we engage with each other at work, hopefully you'll get something out of my own personal mistakes. Someone should.

CHAPTER 1

THE GIANT MINUS
Mob Rule

I've never been to rehab or AA, but I've seen enough TV shows where they always say the same thing: the first step to solving a problem is admitting you have one. (I would assert that the first step is actually to acquire the problem, but whatever.)

And in the case of this book, it's true: in order for us to become better people, we have to identify what makes us inherently bad. Once we do that, we can choose a better path. And what makes us bad is schadenfreude. No, it's not just speaking German that makes us bad, although that helps; it's that we take pleasure in the unfortunate problems that afflict people more successful than we are, as if their success is a temporary aberration standing in the way of our own success. I'd like to think I'm better than this, but even I feel a dopamine rush when I read about the embarrassing predicament a peer of mine finds himself, or herself, in. I don't like admitting this, but I know it to be true. The key is admitting it, and then vowing to resist it.

This is where I am going to use an example close to home. Back in October 2018, Megyn Kelly was heavily criticized for comments she made on her relatively new NBC show (remember, she'd left FNC for a massive pile of money to helm a morning show called *Megyn Kelly Today*—an amazingly innovative title, I admit). The comments were about whether blackface could be acceptable as part of a Halloween costume. It ignited a media, and then social media, firestorm—the kind that can't be extinguished because there's such a low bar for its participation. In the old days, you had to go outside and buy pitchforks to organize a mob. Now you can do it all from a couch (organize a mob, that is, and with a click, Amazon will deliver a case of pitchforks for sixty-nine bucks). It's now super-easy to galvanize 150,000 outraged voices sitting in bathrobes in their spartan apartments, easier than it is to corral twenty villagers to chase a horse thief out of town. Worse, it's also really easy to get maybe a hundred lonely people to sound like 150,000 outraged voices, who easily scare the crap out of the skittish bosses.

After Kelly made her unfortunate comment, she sent out an internal email apologizing for the remarks. Apparently co-workers were deeply upset (more over her massive contract than her clueless defense of blackface, I'm betting). So she went on the air and cried through another apology—humiliating for her, since she was fired anyway. It was gross because almost nobody defended her. Me included. We just watched. Because in the current climate of cancel culture, no one wants to insert themselves between the mob and their target of wrath. So, you just watch it unfold, and hope you burned all those pictures of you from a certain mid-eighties costume party when you dressed as a little-person version of Mr. T.

Of course we felt very bad. But we saw it unfold and in our collective heads thought "it could be us, but better her than me." It's even weirder when you see how Canadian prime minister Justin Trudeau walked through a scandal of a minimum three documented blackface moments. Why was Kelly scapegoated, and not him—or that creepy governor of Virginia, Ralph Northam, who may have dressed either in blackface or like a Klansman for his yearbook photo (our fearless journalists, who bravely chase down people who post memes, never really got to the bottom of that, did they)?

Perhaps it's because both Trudeau and Northam had the seal of approval granted by a media that shared their political stances. As long as you express the right beliefs, you'll have defenders. If you don't fit that description, then you won't. A great example: how the media gave Northam a pass, but not the twenty-plus thousand pro-gun demonstrators in his state who in January 2020 came to protest new gun control laws. The establishment media flagged the gathering as mostly white supremacists (which included many *real* black faces).

Anyway, people took pleasure in Kelly's downfall. And maybe I followed the spectacle a little more than I should have, because I need to be reminded that what exists in others exists in me. People are petty and mean—and I'm considered a person, barely. In a life of less-than-fine moments, this was certainly among them.

It's a fact that you can ruin me, and I can probably ruin you. We are all sinners. We make mistakes. We hope they'll be buried and forgotten. But sooner or later, all mistakes come to the surface. If you think you're safe now—give it time. You're going to do something by accident (tweeting when you thought you were texting, etc., and what were you doing with that pickle?), and then you'll quickly get sucked into the swirling cone of shame, only to be spit out when the public finds another person to publicly humiliate. It could happen on a smaller scale—

just among friends and family, for instance. But your time in the barrel will come. If you even touch social media, you'll soon learn that your fifteen years of shame is the price of your nanosecond of fame.

WHY DO WE JOIN A MOB?

All of today's major societal problems are based on a need to make a difference that cannot be satisfied spiritually. Now, I'm not talking people in third-world countries, or lawless nations where Twitter feuds are the least of their problems. I'm talking about here. The West, and specifically, America.

Because we have mostly solved the basic problems (food, clothing, shelter), and because the pursuits that remain (sports, entertainment, sex, Yahtzee) are now democratized and bottomless, so we are left with a new problem: Instagram. It turns out that we are all the same, except for those whose imprint is larger. That's not a shoe size, it's a social status. How big is your social footprint? Ask Instagram. Because society has *instagrammed* your worth. The number of followers dictates your value. And if that sort of fame is not present in your lifetime, then for those left bitter and alone, infamy is the next-best thing.

In other words, a huge but meaningless part of your life is actually under your control. You can collect likes or encourage hates. If hate is what you're best at, good news: we now place an enormous value on notoriety, one that even Twitter can't satisfy. Some of the darker souls on this planet realize that it's far easier to shoot thirty people and live for years in press clippings and documentaries, than tweet a thousand times to an empty void. In terms of simple return on investment, it's much easier to be Jeffrey Dahmer or the Joker than Norman Borlaug. The fact that you know the first two people better than the third says something (look him up—he's saved more lives than the Red Cross). If you know neither, then welcome, my Martian reader. It's a dangerous environment when the world creates an instant reward for instant fame. Some of us are willing to grab that check and cash it. If you are really craven and evil, Hollywood will make a movie about you, then blame guns for evildoing, and not their own glorification of nihilism.

Perceived inequality is the polio of modern life, except there's no vaccine for it. It's now everywhere you look, when before it was invisible. This intensifies a personal emptiness that sees as its only solution a public display of something, or anything. It can drive you into the arms of a mob, or perhaps worse—to a place outside all human contact where a violent spectacle becomes preferable.

Meanwhile, those who are more charming and better-looking than some of us command greater real estate in the world of social media. Before Tinder, a plain guy with a decent personality had at least a small chance; he didn't need a map to find a gym; he worked on his barroom patter and took up hobbies like skydiving, hoping that such things could overtake a lack of hair, height, or hedge funds. You could see homely guys at bars doing pretty good. Not anymore. Because who goes to a bar to meet anyone these days (I sure don't, I can't emphasize that enough), unless you've already set it up through an app? (It's tough for single people: it's frowned upon to date coworkers, but the "dating scene" outside work is so grim. Could it be it's hurting both sexes when we now view every flirtation as the gateway to predatory behavior?)

Digital dating has eliminated that path and created a methodology biased toward those who already have a physical advantage. The majority of decisions made—swipe left, swipe right—are almost entirely evolutionary: height, weight, symmetry, status. Perhaps 10 percent of the men now command the affections of half the women—who aren't complaining. Women would rather compete for an affluent, high-status male than settle for the guy who may not own a beach house, but knows the difference between Plato and Plotinus or can change a tire in the rain. The internet has eliminated "getting to know someone."

Is this really all that bad? While we see a recent overall decline in basic criminal behaviors (you can cite a number of factors for this, but that's for another book and one I haven't received a cash advance for), we also see more verbal, public, online outbursts, probably because such platforms for exposure didn't exist before. Of course, I'll take an online tantrum over a violent mugging anytime, and do—but it's worth investigating the cruel streak appearing among strangers in a strange world. The internet, strangely, now connects us too much. I'm on a first-name basis with the ids of people I will never meet in person. And it's too easy to forget that there is a reason you would never meet them in person.

What if you have a disorder that needs fixing? Like, maybe you believe that your healthy left leg is evil and needs removal? It's all you think about! Before social media you'd likely be placed in a mental hospital, and hopefully someone would figure out how to talk you out of this delusion. Now, on the Web, you can find a thousand people who feel the same way about their own left leg. What was once considered a disorder is now considered a club. What's wrong with you becomes something worth championing.

THE MOB'S NEW BEST FRIEND: SOCIAL MEDIA

Cruelty within social media cuts across all ages, sexes, and ethnicities. It even appears among both believers and atheists. Therefore, it's not a problem that can be tackled with spiritual renewal, because the problem afflicts both the godless and the godful.

You want proof of this? Okay, here's some science that really isn't science at all—it's just me looking at the avatars of the most annoying offenders on Twitter. I always check the bios of those who denigrate the looks of others, or unload brutal insults on me or a friend. I have found that religion plays no role—in fact, agnostics and the religious can be equally petty. God or no God—we all engage in jerky behavior. Hypocrisy is the unifying factor—for it seems those who preach tolerance (the agnostic approach to religion) and forgiveness (the Christlike avenue) can make fun of your weight or forehead crease equally. Social media levels the playing field in making us all blithering fools. (By the way, I'm not entirely against such body-shaming: it got me to lose weight, and get a new haircut.)

I've said this before: Twitter is the modern bathroom wall, where we can breathlessly scrawl any number of gross ideas anonymously.

But we also tend to treat the outside world within social media like an ex. It's true: nearly every post we deliver possesses this underlying emotional plea that seems to scream, "How do you like me now?" Its like we're trying to prove something to someone out there who hurt us, once. And we want them to let us know they heard us. They don't. Instead we get the weirdos who think our thighs are too fat (it's a family trait, so let it go).

Naturally, this need for approval drives attention-seeking: everyone on Twitter is vying for likes and retweets, doing all they can to make an impact, and if not that, just to be recognized as existing. Every day, anxious attention-seekers attach themselves to a make-believe causes ("This person made a joke about fat kids and deserves punishment!" "I'm boycotting Chik-fil-A over their stance on camels!" "If there is no female James Bond, I'm no longer bathing!") so they can easily measure their impact against others. It's wonderful in that everyone gets a megaphone; it's horrible in that the noise is deafening. And this brings out the worst from people that you might have loved growing up, and now wished you'd never hear from again. Alyssa Milano and her insistence that high schoolers wearing red MAGA caps are like Klansmen is an example of how the need for approval can turn a once-appealing actress into a tragic cartoon.

Meanwhile, as certain crimes decline and social media worsens, our lives are grimly punctuated by spectacle shootings that reopen wounds just weeks after we artificially heal them. The drive for infamy, propelled by the certainty that the press will cover one's actions incessantly, almost like you actually matter, turns a morbid action into an appealing one, at least for a handful of fiends. There is, apparently, no longer a difference between famous and infamous. And either can get you trending on Twitter. We call these fiends monsters, but they're just chasing the spotlight we give them.

MY MISTAKE WITH THE MOB

I like to think I'm smart, discerning . . . an eagle-eyed skeptic. But I'm also a sucker for a story, and I can be as easily tricked as the next guy into joining a mob. I can't believe it, but yep, it's true. Take that Covington kid story.

First, I firmly believe that Saturdays are the worst days for making decisions. It's when I'm at my most vulnerable, career-wise. Meaning, it's my day off and I'm drinking.

I often spend Saturday at a bar having a lazy, leisurely lunch (I refuse to say "brunch"—a word created for jerks who can't decide when to eat, nap, or work; it's like "dinfast," when you pass out on your steak and wake up for coffee and eggs), and where I'll be putting a sizable dent in both a bottle of wine and the patience of my "friends" (that is, the bartender and waitresses). Meanwhile, my wife is at Pilates, which is stretching for people with money.

At the bar, I am pleasant to be around. I tip well. I am on top of the world, for roughly three hours. But then I make that stupid mistake: I go online. I check Twitter, because I'm waiting for the next drink, or my buddy went to buy a panda, and I don't know how to sit still.

It is then that I am at my weakest. I usually bring the laptop, in case I want to write something—and usually I do. I write constantly—most of it is total brilliance—until I get home, give it a once-over, and delete everything. This is why Twitter sucks. Once what you post is out there, there are no second chances. Even deletion makes it more obvious that it warrants scrutiny. It's really the height of idiocy for me. I rail against the idea of Twitter, because I give them content for free. Content that they can sell, but that could get me fired—which is far more likely than the content I get paid for. And yet, knowing that, I go on Twitter . . . drunk. It's the equivalent of saying, "Don't play with guns," and then holding a pay-per-view of me jumping out of a biplane buck naked holding a loaded AK-47. And all the money goes to someone I hate (my cousin, Steve).

And so on one Saturday, mildly drunk, I committed the crime I accuse others of doing. I fell for a media narrative. And after falling for it, I tweeted. I felt that I had no choice but to tweet! I had to let the world know how I felt! It was like I had to piss and it was seventy-five miles to the next rest stop. I had to get my virtue signaled, and immediately.

This is something I mock everyone else (including you) for doing. I spend long moments on *The Five* admonishing viewers never to worry about being "first" on any news story. No matter how hot your super-hot take is, write it down on a piece of paper, crumple it up, and then, in an act of total plusness, eat it. Within minutes you'll forget you ever had the idea. That tweet that you swore was the smartest thing ever written since the *What's Happening* episode about bootlegging will be behind you. Soon you will have the most disturbing bowel movement since that time in third grade when you ate four crayons on a dare. (Burnt sienna tastes like it looks.)

Yet one Saturday in January, I totally disobeyed my brilliant rule. It was January 18, 2019, to be precise (thanks, Wikipedia, for always being there when my memory isn't). On that day rallies for the March for Life were taking place. And a group of Covington Catholic high School students were hanging around at the National Mall, near the Lincoln Memorial, waiting for the bus ride home.

This was their first mistake. An annual school trip to attend a pro-life rally makes you an awesome target for just about anyone who has time to kill, once they're done with the fetuses. You want to create an army of online enemies? Let people know you're at a pro-life rally. Runner up: let 'em know you're speaking at one (and you're pregnant).

You know what happened next. A group of Native American marchers confronted the grinning kids. (The kids were wearing MAGA hats, no less—which, by the way, illustrates a key point about the Trump phenomenon: young people do shocking things as a form of rebellion. Today, wearing the MAGA hat *is* that rebellion; it's worth a dozen Che T-shirts. In fact, everyone trying to act dangerous can't even match wearing a Trump hat for its ability to say "up yours" to our coddled culture. It's the new Hells Angels jacket. But in ten years, they'll be everywhere, worn by hipsters striving for irony. I wonder, will this upset President Ivanka?)

The encounter was caught on tape. What the tape was missing before this encounter were the Black Hebrew Israelites, who had initiated this bizarre event by engaging the teens. Most—if not all—the people who had latched on to the story had no idea about that previous encounter (including me), and that this group had kicked this whole mess off to begin with. The story, however, became about one teen only—Nicholas

Sandmann, who appeared to be grinning at a lone Native American activist, a Vietnam vet, according to nearly every media report, named Nathan Phillips, as he solemnly played his drum. That was what our nation's capital's smartphones captured, and that instant narrative was what the media embraced; that's what was uploaded to the social media universe to be viewed by millions of bored and conflict-seeking and anger-aroused people (including again, me—who had already digested two-thirds of a bottle of rosé—and if you think I'm using that as a defense, you're damn straight I am, although I should have probably changed "rosé" to something slightly more masculine, like "a pitcher of mimosas").

The story exploded on Twitter, like crap in a burning sack on your front porch; a minute-or-so video of a bunch of smirking teens surrounding a solitary Native American with an old-guy ponytail, obviously mocking him. What a lesson for all of us: the larger the story became, the less any facts mattered. Suddenly the whole story had "minus" written all over it. The story became a black hole, sucking everyone, including me, in.

I played the video, and in my haze, made that calculation that everyone does: "This looks awful. And because these brats are—quote—*on my side*—unquote—they will tarnish all of us!" The strategy, which is not an unsound one, is to police your own group, so you appear balanced when you police *the other side.* So I tweeted something about how these damn kids should apologize. That way, when I go after jackasses on the left, the response that I'm an ideologue will fall flat—I can simply point out how I criticized these bratty little brat-faces.

But, as it happened and as I should have predicted, my response was mild compared to others.

Twitter had become a ticker tape of rabid condemnations: celebrities demanding these teens be doxed, media making broad pronouncements once again about Trump's America. Prominent leftists suggested nothing short of violence toward these kids as a response.

So as this story spread like lice all over the thin skin of social media, the anger was uniformly targeted at the kids, especially Sandmann, and their school—resulting in death threats for these smirking jerks. The story became the perfect symbol for a media that loves perfect symbols and simple stories. The incident, to the media, was the epitome of all that was wrong with a racist, Trump-poisoned America—an "explosive convergence," in a *New York Times* phrase—of race and religion. The outrage cycle hit full bore. The mob grabbed a rope and made for the tree. Everyone joined in, from the *Washington Post* to the *New York Times*, to Vox to your habitually enraged celebs. Jim Carrey sprinted to his canvases (he paints now, as therapy for being an asshole) and unleashed a piece of execrable art portraying the students as vile "baby snakes." Kathy Griffin spent her free time (of which she has lots) tracking down a picture of Covington basketball players making Nazi signs! (Turns out it was a symbol players make with their fingers when a three-pointer is made—something most people would have realized if they weren't bat-shit crazy, or Kathy Griffin.) Alyssa Milano, whose tweets always carry the wisdom of the canary, said Sandmann's MAGA cap was the modern Klan hood. She said this in a tweet, hashtag: #FirstThoughtsWhenIWakeUp. See?

I could laugh at them, and they'd deserve it. They were complete minuses, taking a combustible event and happily fanning the flames. But I had also played my small part in the hysteria, too. And that embarrasses me. Which is why I must always include this error whenever I write about theirs. If not, I'd be a hypocrite and a liar. And I can't expect the media to learn from its mistakes, if I don't admit my own.

At first, when I saw the cropped, edited video of the drumming and the kids—I responded as many did. I saw the thing, and said, "Wow, those kids are being jerks. They should apologize and maybe get spanked!"

That tweet still exists, by the way: I didn't delete it. I don't believe in deleting anything, even if it's wrong. I do believe in making restitution, which is what I did, almost immediately. When I saw the real story unfolding, I confessed my error. I also used my platform at FNC—on *The Five* and *The Greg Gutfeld Show*—to expose my own folly while defending the real victims: the Covington kids.

But for those kids, the mob was already in motion. You had the consensus media—their latest anti-Trump story ready to translate into eyeballs and advertisers who bank on the outrage churn. The *Washington Post* led the way, and why not: this was a perfect story. I mean, consider all the fantastic ingredients:

- a bunch of mostly white Southern teens—which is three strikes already. Teens by nature are gross and obnoxious. They smell, they're clumsy, and they take up room. Southerners—well, we know about them. And being white makes them even more guilty. In fact just being born makes them guilty. Which is hilarious given . . .

- It was happening at a right-to-life march. And we know how the media feels about those who care about the rights of unborn people.

- They were wearing "Make America Great Again" caps. If you haven't received the Milano memo, it is akin to wearing a white hood and robe. But actually it's worse than that. You probably drive a pickup. With a *rifle rack*. (And worst of all, you vote for candidates who can win.)

- The so-called victim was Native American—which allowed him to control the narrative from the start. I mean, if you're the *Washington Post*, who are you going to believe—some awful white kids from Kentucky (Catholics, no less!), or this lone elderly Native American?

Two things, in combination, made the Covington smear work: The swarm of hate against the teens was a social media phenomenon—but it was orchestrated by the consensus-driven, activist press. One was the horse, but the other had the whip.

This is when I realized you can't just blame Twitter or Face-book. They're just platforms there for the taking. They can be a plus or minus. It's not the platform spreading the story. It's the media—whose idea of "reporting" is to read tweets and dump the lies into the garbage truck that is modern newspapers and blogs. Twitter was merely the vehicle for the toxic Big Gulp the media created. Fact is, you need a reputable force to make the story real, and that isn't social media. Finding stuff takes time, even for the *Washington Post*, and that may mean no lunch. So the establishment media resorted to social media to give the narrative sufficient gravity, before it was unleashed. (As I write this, the news broke that CNN settled with Sandmann over his lawsuit filed against them; no one outside the courtroom knows what the settlement actually is, but I'm hoping Nick got enough cash to buy a house across from Jeff Zucker, just to moon him every morning.)

Working inside the media, and standing outside of it, I see it for what it is. It's a narrative-making machine, and it alone chooses the direction the machine takes. After watching how fast the Jeffrey Epstein saga evaporated after his death, I realized that the media picks and chooses its stories, and decides when to let them go, or turn up the juice. You can feel the gears shifting, with almost any story. Why did the Epstein story disappear, but the Covington story explode? (Answer: one implicates people they liked, the other destroys people they hate.) It's no wonder the media's popularity among the public ranks similarly to scurvy among pirates.

But my lesson of rushing to judgment is your lesson now, and it led me to a solution that guides me in almost all decisions.

THE PLUS VS. THE MOB

The bigger the dustup, the longer you must stay away. Now when I look at a story, I close my laptop and wait. Hours later, if I still feel strongly about something, or at least enough to discuss it, I ask myself this question: Is what I am adding to this story, a plus . . . or a minus? What if it's neither? When I look at that Covington tweet I posted, I simply added my weak voice to a cacophony of weak voices. It was only when I admitted I was wrong that I turned it into a plus.

If I had asked myself this question—will this next act be a plus or a minus—that Saturday afternoon *before* I tweeted about the Covington kids, I never would have tweeted at all. I would have waited. But I didn't—because I'm a cheap carny whore to my ego. I am insecure, so I had to be first. I wanted people to hear *my* voice so they knew I was normal and not crazy. I was like Liz Warren in seventh-grade English, wildly waving her hand with the right answer first. If I had simply asked myself that simple question first—Is this a plus or a minus?—that choice in stark terms would have kept me from joining in with the braying mob.

In fact, if I had asked this question before a lot of things I've done in my life, I'd have more pluses than minuses in my life—and fewer neighbors pooping in my garden.

The Plus question I always ask myself is this: Is what I'm about to write publicly really that important? (The answer is almost always a big fat no.)

When you screw up, apologize with verve. When I realized I had jumped the gun on Covington, I didn't just jump back, I performed restitution. I asked myself: how do I turn this minus back into a plus, for the kids and myself? I covered the event on both TV shows with monologues, and wrote a piece on it. My goal was to do the opposite of what is traditionally done with screwups—instead of playing it down, I wanted to play it up.

As a reminder to myself, and to others.

THE PLUS VS. BOOZE AND SOCIAL MEDIA

Put it away when you're putting it away. Blaming bad tweets and other stuff on alcohol is a great excuse. Because it makes sense and is usually spot-on. But is it fair? To answer that question: my team at Gutfeld Labs covered our Speedos with white coats and conducted a number of experiments. Here's the study summary: yes.

I have found comparing sober tweets to buzzed tweets and found absolutely *no* difference in quality. They are identical in humor and smarts. But while the difference isn't in quality, there is a wide gulf in quantity. I just tweet more when I'm drunk. Which means the effects of alcohol are not in the nature of the tweets but in the increased risk of publishing them.

It's like playing in traffic. Doing it once is bad. Doing it twice is twice as bad. Unless you're killed the first time.

Sober tweets sound exactly like drunk tweets, but you just generate more tweets when drunk. So what's missing isn't wit or brevity, but restraint. Tweeting drunk merely enlarges the target for those who are bored and aiming at you to indulge their aimlessness and cost you your job. It's not about quality, but quantity. You won't die if you bungee jump once, but ten times a day for a month straight . . . it's a distinct possibility.

It shouldn't come as a surprise, but booze and spontaneity aren't a healthy combination. In the old days, it led to a lampshade on your head and trying to kiss an office mate at the company party. Thanks to the internet and a potential audience of thousands, it leads to a hangover that literally can't be beat.

Which leads me to a bigger point about life.

Drugs and alcohol: both operate as obliviators (often resulting in bloviating). Because they pull you out of your world—defined by periods of anxiety, worry, dread, pointlessness—you in effect change yourself for the worse. You become your own evil twin.

You've heard comments made about certain friends or relatives.

"He's a nice guy, but don't get him drunk."

"She gets really mean after a few."

"Whenever he drinks, he does that thing with his epiglottis."

Intoxication allows you to see the change in you. Which proves that consciousness is biological—because no soul would be vulnerable to tequila.

It's pretty easy, it seems, to change who you are, and in an effort to be a better person you become someone else. The problem is, that someone else maybe the worst person on earth. What if you aim for Dennis Prager but end up Tom Arnold? Mistakes happen and sometimes they even get work.

So the question becomes, as a drinker and a druggie: Are you a plus or a minus when you pull the trigger of oblivion? Are you happy or mean—or a bit of both (which still sucks)? I think I can master this tricky world, but only if I can see the change in myself *before* it appears to others. Once you can sense a shift in your behavior, or trust those who see it and ask you to have a glass of water, then you can learn to reap the benefits of oblivion without ruining an evening. Or your pants.

THE PLUS: CALL YOUR OWN TRUCE

If your life seems like warfare and you want to find peace, don't signal your virtue. Hide it! Yes, of course you are a superior person. Buying this book proves that. But not everyone is as smart as you are, so instead of tweet-beating others, take a walk. *Nothing you say will convince anyone of anything.* The media may be irritating, but that doesn't mean they are as powerful as they'd like to think. Look back at 2016 for evidence. In fact, it's the refusal by the media to believe that people no longer have trust in them that motivates their extremism. So why bother refuting some half-baked claim made by somebody you don't know in a tweet?

Here's a reply that will infuriate them more than your heavily researched rejoinder: "That's interesting." It's a perfectly neutral response that will surely irritate your adversary, but one that will allow you to go to lunch and get on with your day, certain that you've shown that you're not as minus as your Twitter-enemy. In fact, you're Plus-Plus.

THE PLUS: PRESET EVERY RESPONSE TO FORGIVE

If you adjust your dial to "forgive," you'll carry fewer burdens. It's hard to remember everyone you're mad at, so here "forgive" really does mean "forget." Just remember you will likely not get the same treatment in return.

I accept apologies as easily as I accept money. In fact, it is a currency. You accept it, and that offending party feels grateful, and owes you one. So it's not necessarily money you can spend right away—it's like that sockful of coins you buried under that weird-looking rock by the grave you dug for your first—and last—guinea pig. It might come in handy someday. Again, I accept apologies knowing this will not be reciprocated. But I say the time is ripe to take that step, even if it's unilateral, toward forgiveness.

It's why I forgive, even when I know I may not get it in return (yet). I am working toward a concept that I have called MAF—Mutually Assured Forgiveness. Meaning if I forgive Joy Behar for crapping on Christians or for being born stupid, she'll forgive me when I call her a flesh-eating smog monster on Twitter, even though I know she wouldn't. In fact, I will forgive anyone, hoping that one day they will forgive me. It might not happen at that very moment, but every time I forgive someone, it gives me that opportunity to explain the concept and bribe a few converts.

So every time someone screws up, you can turn their minus into a plus for both of you. Just accept all apologies immediately but keep notes. The dividend may not appear right away, but in time it could accrue, and help you in time of need (when the notes also will be handy). It sounds a little selfish, I guess, to forgive, hoping that others do the same for you—but it beats the alternative: to ruin those first who might ruin you later.

THE PLUS: VICE SIGNAL

Mad genius Eric Weinstein recently coined a phrase called "vice signaling"—an ugly but necessary method to combat the roving mobs of virtue signalers, who use their own manufactured moral outrage to elevate their status. Vice signaling has you confess your own vile practices before anyone can out you for the same sins. Basically, you're committing character hara-kiri before some career failure at a blog can claim your scalp for himself. I did this a lot, before I knew there was a name for it. On my old show, *Red Eye*, I happily alluded to rampant drug use, bizarre sexual practices, and lurid crimes committed in my past—and sometimes present (all patently false, of course! I cannot stress that enough). I spoke of midnight dog-walking in parks without a dog; meeting "workout partners" at the Port Authority bus station; creating an "activity pit" in my basement designed for drifters and runaways (which by the way, became the name of a *Red Eye* fan club). I'd been vice signaling for years—without knowing there was a name or a reason for it.

As Weinstein said to me, it sucks that to protect yourself from ruin, you must ruin yourself first, publicly (it's like knocking yourself out before being decked). But it works. Perhaps vice signaling has built a little moat around me that keeps the busybodies at bay. I think it has, in part, albeit temporarily. But I am aware it is never enough; someone is always watching and waiting for me to screw up. There are at least three or four miserable wretches who chronicle my daily TV appearances, clipping segments that might bring me down professionally, and personally (they're members of my family, so that makes it uncomfortable around the holidays).

THREE-PLUS QUESTIONS

Every choice is a coin flip: plus or minus? Command yourself every morning to choose a positive path and eliminate anything that can be seen as a minus. You want three questions that'll help you separate the plus from the minus? Well, here they are!

- If something horrible happened in the news, would what you say on social media make it less horrible? If you can't see that outcome, then skip. That's a plus. No need to express publicly what has already been said by people less thoughtful than you. Public opinion is a landfill you don't need to unload in.

- Are you in a bad mood? Before you make any decision, ask yourself, "How am I feeling?" My dumbest actions are usually dictated by my moods, which change hourly. If I wait a mood out, the urge always goes with it. So before you're about to give that customer service rep a peace of your mind, check to see if it's an angry piece of your pissed-off mind that's making you do this. A deep breath beats a hot take, and you can quote me on that.

- Is what you're about to do driven by boredom and the promise of novelty? Novelty informs most decisions you later regret, and once you see that, you can scoot right past that last shot of Sambuca and the girl trying to get you to suck it out of her belly button. (Her name is really Frank, and that's not her belly button.)

THE OPPOSITION TOXIN

I've interrupted my research on the causes of involuntary eye rolling at Gutfeld Labs to spend some time trying to pinpoint the exact problem behind life's unraveling social fabric.

I call it the opposition toxin. It's when any relationship, idea, or event is transformed into an "us vs. them," or "me vs. you," or hell, "X vs. Y" paradigm.

I think I've figured the whole thing out—and I want to share it with you, using a story that made news around Christmas 2019.

Now, this story isn't anything special. It's just a small example of how the oppositional toxin works.

You remember Peloton, right? (Don't answer: I can't hear you.) Peloton is a successful company that sells sleek exercise bikes, coupled with online classes featuring trainers/cyclists who run their classes while offering pep talks along the way, like a propaganda parrot perched on your shoulder. I don't think you'll find a more positive skill set than among the average Peloton instructor. Not only are they super-fit, they're relentlessly positive—and highly trained in persuading anyone to do better. These people deserve credit for working against the current societal grain plagued by victimology. They dare you to improve instead of blame.

So, in a commercial for their exercise bike, which hit social media before Thanksgiving 2019, titled "The Gift That Gives Back," a husband gives his grateful wife a Peloton bike. She then spends every day, for the next *year*, creating a video diary of her progress. And then thanks her husband for the gift that changed her life.

The ad quickly became a target of ridicule in social media, especially from East and West Coast hacks, all of whom could use a loving spouse, or a few hours on a bike. The video was criticized for depicting a woman so beholden to her husband that she had to get in shape—or else face some imaginary, dark punishment. Some writers implied that the husband was an abuser because his wife looked "a little nervous."

The weeklong controversy over this commercial illustrates what Scott Adams calls the "two movies on one screen" phenomenon. In sum, it's when two people can watch the same thing, and see two entirely different stories.

So here you have a commercial, in which the creators intended a selling point being a woman grateful for a gift from her husband that greatly improved her health—and *both their* lives. That's key: they're in this together; they're a team; they're married. Not adversaries, but side by side. Because she's healthier and happy, and he is too. It's pathetic that we have to explain this, but so be it. It's what happens when you're part of a team, whether that team is a husband and wife, a company, a classroom.

Yet, one group of people (surprise—media people and Twitter losers; often one and the same) saw it differently. They saw it as a woman driven by fear of her abusive husband to exercise until she was anorexic.

So, it became two movies seen on one screen.

But what causes this double vision?

I call it the opposition toxin: the inclination for the media, academia, and entertainment industries to see two groups, or individuals, as always in conflict. Men vs. women; black vs. white; gay vs. straight; left vs. right. That simple equation allows for the production of an endless supply of opposition toxin, otherwise known as "news content"—especially if the writer of such content has an agenda, a lack of humor and goodwill, and a limited imagination (and these often go together).

Do you want to see how this toxin can change a simple story into something polluted? Then the Peloton commercial is perfect.

Here is a summary of the commercial, minus the opposition toxin: *A wife receives an expensive exercise bike from her husband. She is grateful for the gift and for his support in maintaining good health; he is happy that she is pleased. They are in this little effort together!*

Now add the opposition toxin: *The bribe reflects the incurable, patriarchal tension between the sexes; the man is enforcing his desire for an attractive, submissive woman who responds fearfully to his orders. Her face tells you that she's oppressed. She's being trafficked on a bike going nowhere.*

Opposition toxin can infect nearly every aspect of your life, if you want it to. You too can become a victim, somebody deserving sympathy and support. And it's powerful—think about what it did to a simple commercial. It turned a basic premise into a feminist dystopia. And everything these days seems to be a feminist dystopia— even as more women get college degrees than men do, field more opportunities than ever before, and essentially kick the men's asses in life span and other barometers of illness. But without the nightmarish lie that pushes division between the sexes, what would the media do? They can't go home to their spouses, clearly.

Did the commercial speak to me at all? No. But it did

to my wife. She told me she wanted the bike for Christmas. And I went out and bought her one. So what does that make me? A sweet and obedient husband doing just what his wife told him to do. In other words, *the real* victim.

CHAPTER 2

WE SEE EVERYTHING AND WANT TO BE SEEN BY EVERYONE

Back at the ranch otherwise known as Fox, we once covered a study reporting that people felt fame was a more important factor in happiness than family or work. In other words, your wife and kids could hate your guts, but if the waiter recognized you from that thing you did on TikTok with the electric toothbrush and a hamster, that made your night (especially if you got a free drink out of it).

To the people like me who pay attention to the need for attention, this finding is utterly predictable, but no less horrifying.

Without much effort, we've turned life into a global competition for attention. We'll do anything to win. But it wasn't always like this.

When I was growing up, I lived three houses down from Jamie Jones (a fake name, so don't bother googling). We were the same age, in the same class—and I had no idea if he had more friends or more toys than me. A curtain of unknowing separated us. I never saw his family life, so I had no interest in his family life (maybe he had a mom, dad, a lizard, and perhaps a brother—I remember seeing bunk beds—but that could have been during that time I had to wear an eye patch for double vision), and he seemed a better athlete (a low bar compared to me), but that was never a bone of contention. We were friends, which meant we weren't nosy. Now the world is vastly different. And awful. *We must know all.*

If I were growing up now, I'd be able to know not only everything about Jamie's toy chest and friend supply, but just about any other Jamie on the planet. Famous Jamies, not-so-famous Jamies, Jamies of all different genders and orientations. Even Jamie Farr! (He's still alive, right?) Today, with a gentle tap of my finger, I could find out how much less my dad makes than other dads, just by looking at the posted pics of swimming pools and birthday parties that dwarfed my overgrown back-yard, littered with balloons and paper plates. My family wasn't rich. It wasn't poor. It was just whatever, until my mom's best friend died and left my parents enough of a nest egg to get me and my siblings through college (I was cleared at the inquest).

Now is different, and now it isn't good. The lonely and the alienated and even the not-so-lonely and not-so-alienated now have ample evidence—gigabytes of it, showing how much better off everyone else is. We now can see daily how the world truly treats people differently. And it's not about race, or gender. It's about physical attraction and status. Instagram might have unraveled a few millennia of religion—the serious spiritual attempt to attenuate the realities of the world's natural and brutal unfairness has been destroyed by butt selfies. If religion can't get this ass back in the barn, what can?

We now see everything others have, and we are untethered from the tools that soothe the effects of such differences. Family, community, and religion: what was the three-pronged pleasure principle is now an object of disdain and mockery.

Is it wrong to say that it's loneliness that drives modern politics? Once you see family or community as some sort of lie told to you by "the man," all that's left is political tribalism. You find that social activism replaces the love you might have gotten from those closest to you. Antifa replaces family.

Family, community, and religion: like them or not, for centuries these were the saving concentric circles that protected you—which now social media has leapfrogged over and beyond; it's the HOV lane to a new kind of hell. The barrier to entry is nil, but the arena you enter is ruthless. There's a reason it's free: it's worthless and you pay later. With your data, and your peace of mind.

But before social media ever sprouted its tentacles into every part of your life, postmodernism had already told us to ditch the traditions—without ever having anything better to replace them with. (This is probably why the conversion of Kanye West from hedonistic loudmouth to selfless prophet feels so real and so meaningful: he got to the abyss faster than anyone else on the planet, and is now running back to tell the rest of us how horrible that reality is. He's as close to a real prophet we have these days: he saw it all, and it sucks.)

This is a problem, and it's one that has consequences. But those who know what's coming—otherwise known as experts—don't mind what's coming, and never have. The ideas of alienation and separation are what they had in mind all along. Misery indeed loves company, as certain companies require your misery to exist. CNN, for example.

But if fame is deemed most valuable, and seems to be everywhere yet is elusive or accidental for only a few, then what does that leave you or your children with? Not much—except a persistent emptiness. It leaves you all aching for something that your community used to provide.

Instagram, meanwhile, judges us only by our Darwinian attributes: physical attraction and power. This means that since the Bronze Age, we've progressed only to an even more ruthless class system: literally a social class—one containing beautiful, rich, and young elites who corner the market of every platform.

In the dating world a funny guy could outdo a handsome dullard. A hilarious 6 could outmatch a shallow 10 (here I speak from experience as an amusing 7.2). Not anymore.

Women face different challenges. Women are outgunned by youth, more than anything. Women forget—that for men, it's not about looks. It's about age and newness. That's the driving force behind our selfish genes: forcing men to see in every untapped female a future, be it short-term or not.

Youthful markers are the evolutionary measure and social media reminds us of this daily—forcing females over age thirty into the mimetic hell of cosmetic surgery, where every woman tries to look like every other woman they believe is "youthful." And you end up with faces as tight as the skin on bongos.

Sadly, the world is for the young, and the young have no idea what to do with it. Yeah, I know Oscar Wilde had a far better way of saying that, but he's dead and I'm writing this book, not him, so his version's wasted. (I think it was Wilde who said it. Maybe it was George Bernard Shaw? Either way I always confuse my Belgian writers.)

A sense of obscurity—minus the buffers of family, community, and religion—creates a pathway for the worst kind of psychological disease: a sense of worthlessness that screams for attention. Godlessness means God on earth wins. And how do you keep score? I think we've figured this out. Is it any wonder, on Twitter, people are called "followers"? That sounds meaningful but I got lucky. Fact is, the impossibility of fame ends up pointing you to the possibility of infamy.

That encourages the very worst of human traits—if you can't be famous, you can always be infamous. Nothing narrows the timeline from lonely Saturday to school shooter like this does. Especially as the media creates an ever-expanding spotlight for them—proving that infamy is there for the taking. As the coverage goes wall to wall, like demonic clockwork another attempted mass shooting takes place. One alienated creep sees the reward for such actions, so he copies it.

Modern terrorists take a similar career path. Having no real impact in life, they see apocalyptic war, or a crusade for vengeance against Western decadence, as the alternative. It provides infamy, and within that, eternal life. Truly those guys are the original incels. Their hygiene doesn't help, either.

Infamy is easy, forever, and contagious. Anybody can do it,

and so can a nobody. Fifty years ago, if I decided to walk out into the street and do something awful, it would stay there, likely ended quickly by a cop with fists the size of small cars. Now if I do something awful, I may still be dead, but my death will have more power, more "spectacle spread"—since every eyeball will see it expand like a deadly mold all over Twitter.

We should make this kind of path harder to take.

But we live in a two-dimensional world where vicarious mayhem is ubiquitous but real-world consequences may follow. Video games make you wonder what it's like to kill, not just for points, but for real. I'm not going to lie: back in the 1990s, Doom invaded my dreams at night. But not just Doom. Video games, pornography, and drugs cluttered my unconscious. It's an odd thing, how dreams lift experiences that aren't actually real ones at all, and then drive out real things. Porn is merely a menu of novel simulations, like an empty life seen in time-lapse clips: her, then her, then her. Meanwhile, drugs feel like a journey when in fact you rarely leave the couch; and video games concoct fantasies in a world where what's false feels real. The world's great time-wasters seep into all nooks.

Get high, play games, watch porn: it's the modern male triathlon in a universe where options seemed narrowed. The West is becoming the new Sparta. For jerk-offs.

What's missing now, that before had kept this at bay? We sacrificed community, while replacing it with a facsimile that oddly isolates us in our rooms.

But do not fret—I have answers. Or, I pretend to!

THE PLUS

Think of fame as a fire: run, duck, roll.

You're so hot.

No wonder you're sweating and uncomfortable and worried you may be looking fat.

You'll look much slimmer in a new gray cloak of invisibility. Even a little bit of fame is like dating a supermodel. You think, "Oh, this is nice." Then you start getting the bills for maintenance and on your way to debtor's prison (aka "spacious studio apartment"), you suddenly long for the nice, smart woman you used to "date," if that's what you call those squalid, mortifying nights in dives in Queens or New Jersey.

The high cost of fame can be measured in many ways—in money, time, and self-respect. Usually all three. And for what? A tiny spark of recognition when you buy your movie ticket so you can sit in a dark room surrounded by people who aren't at all interested in you? Measure your worth by the people around you who know you, not by the people "out there" who don't.

Treat social media like an acquaintance, not an ex. We go on Twitter and Instagram to show off, generally to some amorphous mass that represents everyone we want to impress. Basically the Web is the last person who dumped you. You must prove them wrong—you are somebody.

Instead, why not treat that world like it really is: some unknown quantity who couldn't care less about your achievements. The people you want to impress aren't there. My guess—those people are in a nearby room wondering what the hell you're up to, locked away for hours stuck in an attention-suck vortex. Which leads me to the easiest, simplest plus of all:

Replace the instinct to reply with physical action. When you're online, and you're about to say a really nice thing to your favorite talk show host named Greg, try this: Get up, and walk to the person closest to you, and transfer that energy to them. Say something that won't get you into trouble. Even a banality like "Have you lost weight?" changes a person's life far more wonderfully than writing nice things to a stranger, even if that stranger is me. It might sound corny, but it's a twofer—it prevents you from saying something foolish in a public space, and forces you to reacquaint yourself with actual conversation. I do this even when alone, by paying myself lavish compliments. Experts call it self-talk but it's basically me mumbling on the subway so no one will sit next to me.

Go out of your way to know less about your neighbors. Don't snoop online. I know it's tempting to google everyone you know—but knowledge ruins everything (I think Einstein said that).

Do the grandmother test. The best way to expose the pointlessness of novelty (and how it ruins stable, fruitful relationships) is to see who you'd never replace in your life. Can you imagine a different mother? A different grandmother? Different sisters? Novelty—that desire for something you've never had before—clouds our relationships with *the unrelated*. But imagine applying that novelty logic to people who exist beyond our evolutionary desires. To family. It won't work. Or it shouldn't work. And that will remind you how illusory and superficial novelty really is. If you don't understand what I'm saying, then just imagine every woman as someone's daughter, and take up bowling.

VIRTUE ETHICS

The whole minus part of life could be made into a plus by embracing what Aristotle called "virtue ethics." It's about avoiding the stuff you just know you shouldn't do. Don't hit your sister. Don't kick the dog. All that until you get to "don't insult interns." It's also the stuff that everyone else on the planet knows you shouldn't do. Killing people, for example, is a global minus, and we don't really need God to tell us so.

The fact that many of us are always on the lookout for ways around the unwritten laws of life gives lawyers all they need to retire rich.

Steal more. The best way to add good things to a rough world is to steal the good things from other people. Meaning, be a wisdom leech. Which is what I am.

When you watch me on *The Five*, you might think to yourself, "How is this young, dashing person so full of amazing wisdom! It's like he's lived nine lives in one—and all without wearing a cat suit!"

Well, yes, it's true, I've lived several lives, at once—simply by surrounding myself with people who are smarter than me in many different areas. So at any moment, when I'm searching for an answer, I can scan my collection of friends and see what I can shoplift from them to turn my current quandary into a plus.

It's funny—as I write this piece of advice about how to steal advice from people around you, I realize that I might have stolen this actual strategy from someone else! (I am not admitting who it is, because I'm not even sure who I stole it from, but I admit, that, unlike daily brushing, this may not be an original Gutfeld idea.)

Being a wisdom leech is not a weakness, though, as long as you give credit to your sources (see above). So, I've got a pretty top-notch menagerie of people who, out of my concern for their modesty, will go nameless here. Some you might know, but many you won't. What's pretty incredible: some of the people giving the best advice are rarely asked for it. So when you do ask, they're super-happy to give it. The best advice I got was from people who didn't even know they were giving it! (I may set that to music—did I mention I own a guitar?)

People love to give advice because it gives them a sense that they've done something worthwhile, without really lifting a finger. In fact, all they did was listen to your question and draw from their past and cultivate a waxy ball of wisdom to toss back at you. When you seem grateful for it, they're almost more grateful. So they throw more. Talk about a double plus: you're getting help by giving help at the same time.

Important note: asking for advice is a good thing, but only if the problem is within what I call "your realm of friendship." That's where you are a princess and where friendship is like pixie dust. Example: don't go to a friend and ask for tips on dumping a body into the East River. That's outside your realm of friendship, unless all your friends are fish. They won't thank you, even though you are only trying to feed them. And you mustn't ever use the opportunity to ask for advice as just an opportunity to solve your own problems, especially if they involve taxes. A friend listens, but even a friend has limits. Only ask them for their ears if you intend to listen to what comes out of their mouths. Friends aren't therapists: they're better than that. They're more like podiatrists.

Remember when you were nothing. Another lesson: good people remember what it was like when they were you. Bad people don't. The best people see what you have or what you're lacking and aren't afraid to challenge you to find it.

One good judge of character is to watch how somebody treats an opening band or comedian. Or a waiter or bartender.

Meaning anyone who stands between that person and what they want. Are they impatient, or are they giving? Do they know what to do in those moments when it looks like they might not get what they want?

Be around people who are nicer than you. This is really easy for me.

CHAPTER 3

DEFEATING THE UNBENDING MIND

Let's say you're calling that toll-free number on the back of your bank card, because you need to do one, simple thing: order more checks.

As you work your way through the automated prompts that almost never hear you the first, second, or third time you repeat the last four digits of your Social Security number, you finally get to a live person, who then proceeds to ask you a series of questions, as a method of preventing someone who might be pretending to be you. (Who in their right mind would pretend to be me? Even I sometimes don't.) What was the middle name of your first parrot? Have you ever visited a foreign country whose president is named after a character in *Hamilton*? Who is your favorite Beatle? (Mine is Mickey Dolenz.) Soon we lose ourselves to our own impatience. We forget that the person on the other side is human—and to be fair, her behavior often doesn't seem like it. But she's doing it for your sake as well as hers.

A common question from that live voice might be to ask you about a recent transaction—a withdrawal, a deposit.

You (or me) cannot think of one.

I rarely use my checking account (my handwriting on a recent check looks like a Geiger counter reading) so I fail to give an exact response. Sometimes I try to initiate an impromptu poetry slam as a substitute. It rarely works. Who are these uncultured rubes?

After four or five tries, the agent denies me access. Freezes my account. No matter what I say or do, I can't reason with her. Because I failed to answer one question, I cannot move forward; I cannot order new checks. I am left sputtering into the phone, reduced to shouting at the lady (I swear she enjoyed it). But the fact is, her denial was nothing personal. It never is. She has a goal, and it's to protect me from not just others, but myself, too.

Still, I felt helpless, because I couldn't reason with this person. The person had something greater in mind than my human need. Her job was predicated on a mission—one that has been programmed into her. The mission: to save the bank money and keep customers safe from theft, by preventing fraud. I understand that, like eating right and flossing regularly, this actually helps me in the long run. But in the short run, I wanted to strangle her with dental floss—and that didn't stop her, either. Not for a second. And even though the goal might have been to prevent fraud, even that is irrelevant to her, for her real goal is to guide me through the hoops she is paid to guide people like me through. She's merely there to enforce the program—a recess monitor who makes sure you do all twenty jumping jacks. Arguing with a bank is like arguing with the weather. That sounds profound even though I am unsure of what exactly it means.

This is now how a fair portion of the population operates at all times. Inflexible, single-lane thinking. Robotic, unpersuadable. It has had a profound impact, in all walks of life.

Consider the meter maid—an obvious human, I think. Her purpose: writing a summons, part of an ambition to surpass her monthly financial nut. That's her goal and there can be nothing to prevent her from reaching it. Her goal means she'll be possibly rewarded with a raise, perhaps a promotion, and maybe a better job that isn't being a meter maid. Like eventually, mayor of New York City. You, dramatically crying to her about only being parked there temporarily to visit your ailing mom, who may or may not be real, mean nothing. Because she cannot let it mean anything. There is no reasoning that works. Her humanity disappears when she's doing her job.

If you've ever been at an airline counter trying to get on a plane in bad weather, you face that unbending mind. The airline's goal: get you there safely and alive, with hopes that you don't end up trending on Twitter by throttling a gate agent. And if you die, they lose customers, status, trust, and future business. That's why they'd rather not fly into that storm you're not worried about because you've had four scotches at the Mexican restaurant where you had to cut your steak with a plastic knife and spilled beans all over your pants and did a screeching Macarena because your crotch was on fire (you will be hearing from my attorney, or at least my dry cleaner). That goal, you surviving another day, is a good one for the airline folks to have. And it trumps your tears, even if your tears are real. You may be trying to make your mother's funeral, or your child's wedding. But their unbending mind, however, is a good thing. It's not a good thing in other places.

Goals beat all things. That can be good in hockey, but evil once you're off the ice. We all come across goal-oriented thinking in every arena of life; it's the ideology that remains rigid and unchanging, a force that is deaf to the pleadings of a human voice. It is an artificial intelligence—a way of achieving an aim that has no actual conscious thinking behind it. It therefore functions separate from a human way of thinking. Goals make us computers. Hell, goals made us invent computers.

Do we have more of this type of thinking than ever? No idea. I do sense that the less power some people have in their lives, the more power they want to exert in their jobs, over you. Meaning, crushing your desires helps ease the pain of their own hopelessness. I have no evidence to back this up, I swear. But I can predict that we all know this type of person when we see them, don't we?

You cannot reason with an unbending mind. The goal of that mind turns you into either a minor speed bump you gently roll over, or an obstacle. It is smarter than you, for it has no need for smarts at all. It has only one mission, and it's the opposite of pragmatic. It's alive in both a machine's voice and a murderer's eyes. When you watch videos of protesters blocking the path of subway trains taking orderlies to hospitals, parents to their sick kids, dads and moms to visit their parents at the home, what you see in the protesters' faces is an unbending mind, as well as a bad case of acne.

The unbending mind lurks everywhere, and once in place is almost unstoppable, sometimes (oftentimes maybe), deadly. Stalin used to have five-year goals for things like tractor production. If your factory didn't meet them, you died.

If you've ever been in a deposition, if you've ever been in a cult, or facing someone who believes in chemtrails, then you might know what I mean. (And you also might know my cousin. We've kind of lost track of him.)

The destructive power of the nonconscious thinking of the robot brain transcends human pleasure or pain. It is the most powerful force in human nature because it's no longer part of it. The desire to complete a result based on a pure belief that one is right can reduce the human brain to a conduit for remorseless action. If you're the torturer, torture is always based on virtue. It is about the virus of ideology, in small and big doses. Ideology is like river blindness, a tropical illness in which tiny parasites enter the body through fly bites, then grow until they emerge through the eyeballs. It's always been here, and once you get it, you can't get rid of it, so it will never go away.

The curse of the unbending mind comes in many shapes and forms. Aside from the ones I mentioned above, there are some more random examples I came up with in the shower:

Witch hunts. If we're going to talk about metaphorical witch hunts, we might as well start with the literal witch hunts: when humans were drowned or torched in bonfires, by other humans—humans who actually knew the poor victims who they were about to kill. They might have been neighbors, but driven by a greater goal—rooting out evil—they dismissed cries for mercy or tepid attempts at reason—and chose to execute. We think this kind of goal-driven mentality is dead (the kind that steamrolls over compassion so horrifically it defies any belief in God), but how does one explain Rwanda, Stalin, Mao, ISIS, or people shopping on Black Friday? In every example, you have to overlook the suffering of others to attain exactly what you want.

Conspiracies. If you've ever fallen into an unintentional conversation with a stranger over chemtrails, or the Illuminati, or worse, with a Holocaust denier, you realize that despite the person being otherwise law-abiding, there is no reasoning with them over these mental potholes. If someone ever uses the phrase "crisis actors" in a discussion, you should flag the waitress and grab your hat. In those cases, reasoning actually works against you. The more wrong a concept is, the more likely a person's attachment to it is a matter of blind faith. Their goal: convince you that the true believer knows something you don't. It's an ego thing. They want you to believe in them, more than anything.

Militant political groups. If you feel you've been wronged by society, and you find thirty others who agree with you, you're no longer a lost soul. You're a movement. In fact, you don't need to be oppressed; you just need to identify an oppressor and appoint yourself the vindictive payback machine. Then run for office in New York or San Francisco.

The revolutionary rarely thinks this all the way through. Saying to them: "Okay, you're right, what's next?" could end up with your pouring this weeping chap into an Uber.

ISIS. As I write this, they have, at least for now, been destroyed. But they could come back (I mean, look at measles!). Or something worse could take its place (like cinnamon-flavored toothpaste). Which raises the question: What makes a young man in the prime of his life accept a death cult that will surely end in his own grisly demise? Obviously maybe they really didn't think the whole thing through. That's usually the explanation for most idiotic decisions (half of all marriages and road trips end for this reason).

To understand ISIS, recall an execution of two Arabs for the "sins" of homosexuality. Before their demise, their executioners hugged them, and they exchanged hugs and words—the killers and soon-to-be killed seemed to understand that this was part of their unbending deal. And they both felt bad about it (well, at least two of them felt *really* bad about it), but according to the zealots with the guns, it had to be done. The ideology—the *goal*, after all—is nirvana, so in a sense, you'll thank me later, gay fellas we're going to kill. The killers are motivated by virtue; they say these men sinned and in death would help them be delivered to their god, free and clean again. When you listen to any member of ISIS, or any extremist death cult, you are no longer listening to a human being—but a dehumanized conduit for ideological software. It is merely a module, working with other modules in a cluster of modules working toward something horrific: a goal that's bigger than all of us.

Looting. Citizens in Baltimore and Ferguson didn't take out their anger on city hall. They burned down their cities' businesses and looted their own neighbor's stores. They destroyed the very places that keep their community alive. Does that person running out of a Kmart really need twenty rolls of toilet paper? Does that dude really think setting fire to a Korean bodega helps his case as a victim of injustice? Can you reason with people as they work against their own interests, violently, and seemingly gleefully? Have you ever tried to talk someone out of doing something stupid that, for the moment, has no immediate consequence? Maybe, if you were the best man, you have. But the mentality of the mob, be it in violent action or mass theft, has its own goal set: destruction. It's like the beginning credits of *Mission: Impossible*: a community of thugs announces it will "self-destruct in sixty seconds," and nothing can turn that around. Goals come before humanity—you see it when business owners plead with these cogs to stop their mechanized assault. Only one time did you see it stop: that moment in Baltimore in 2015, when a mother, on live television, recognized her son participating in some mob action (throwing rocks at police) and berated him in front of his mocking peers. In that one moment, caught on video as the woman smacked the boy and chased him when he tried to walk away, we saw a potential solution: *angry mothers.* Because we've all had one. And frankly, we need a whole lot more of them. My gut tells me that if we ever unleashed the accumulative power of all our angry moms on our ever-degrading culture, they'd get more done than a country-wide army of social workers.

Angry moms could change the world, if they only mobilized!

Drugs. Not all drugs circumvent the desire to survive, but a few of the great ones do. Cocaine, meth, alcohol. It's these drugs that shortcut the usual desires for preservation and long-term thinking. Usually you need to be persuaded or converted to join ISIS, or support a socialist, or beat a man to death you believe to be a warlock. But one hit on the crack pipe and your goals are complete: to get another hit of that crack pipe. The conversion is immediate and absolute. In the 1990s we saw the ground zero of euphoria-as-destination—a phenomenon so powerful it destroyed communities from the inside out. Crack might be the only drug in history that so disgusted people that it was shamed out of existence. Could we learn from that? How did we get people off crack? If you see crack as a determined nonthinking, goal-oriented thing—a software that infects your hardware—how do you exterminate such contaminants? Hint: not with crank.

Artificial intelligence. It's truly artificial, but it's not intelligence by our primitive definition. As expert on this stuff Nick Bostrum predicts, once machines reach super-intelligence, they won't just be smarter than us; they will relegate us to farm animal status. The way we relate to chickens is how our machines will relate to us. They will contain us and ignore us when we beg to go free-range. And their destruction of our entire race will not be personal—any more than our eating of a billion chickens a year is personal (I personally ate that many by myself in 2019). The goals we give AI will be more than enough for them to complete our apocalypse—and they'll be thinking, all along the way, that they're simply doing us a favor by doing what they were told by us to do. As Bostrum points out: ask an AI to perform a simple task—to complete a goal—and they'll interpret that in ways you will never expect. If your AI has been directed by the Dairy Board to assess how much milk is consumed around the world, it could disembowel every human on the planet simply to check our daily intake. And possessed of super-intelligence (think an IQ of say, 70,000), it will be entirely possible for AI to leap, within minutes, to action. And kill everyone for a simple question about milk. It's why I'm lactose intolerant.

SUPER UNBENDING MINDS:
HOW TO READ A NEVER TRUMPER

When Trump skeptics like me were witnessing friends becoming Trump supporters, in our frustrated dismissal we compared them to a cult. The reason for this insult is pretty simple: it answers a question you refuse to honestly ask of yourself. Which is: Why do so many people find this person appealing, but you don't? Rather than spend some time investigating not just their biases but yours, too, you just relegate them all as blind fanatics.

Such a clichéd response is lazy, hacky, predictable, and not helpful, for it overlooks the key reasons real, decent human beings (in your family, no less) find Trump so arresting.

These reasons I've alluded to before in a previous book: Trump is the outsider who came in as a response to decades of bullshit, and in his brash manner, painted the town red. He's the nameless man in *High Plains Drifter*, changing things forever. He was you, if you were put in that position. You'd ask lots of questions, express confusion over red tape and endless team-sport politics, and then shake the box to its very foundations. Trump—love him or hate him—is an undeniable phenomenon—and proof of that is in the response. Those he's threatened— from the generic politician to the establishment media— have led to a frantic response that's beyond extreme. Every day they scream that he's about to lead us into another deadly catastrophe—an apt response for someone who sees their own hold on power being threatened. And they are right only in this sense: Trump threatens to destroy them all.

His goal wasn't unbending; it was positively flexible— its only purpose was to shake the box of a PC world run by complacent elitists who've turned their vocation into a trough. But his opposition was wholly uniform and stiff. He had to be stopped. I know this feeling because I possessed this feeling. It's amazing I escaped it. It felt like I was the one who left a cult.

The unbending nature of Never Trumpism could be a mirror of Pro-Trumpism. But for me—as a man who's been on both sides of it—it's the NTs who seem stuck in a more unbending universe. The NTs might disagree with me—

and who knows, in some cases, they might be right. To be sure, I'm sure they're jerks on both sides.

Nothing makes sense in a Never Trumper's world—the strength of the economy is an anomaly (before the shutdown), the relative lack of war is a fluke, the real improvements in any quality of life are just unexplained phenomena—the calm before the Trump-caused storm. This is not to say that these positive outcomes are due to Trump—it's merely to point out that the predictions of the hell caused by Trump never panned out. How does one explain that? The only way really is to say that the predictive capabilities of the Never Trumper are wholly unreliable, due to their suffocating cognitive dissonance.

How to explain Trump to Never Trumpers: My best analogy for Trump and his effect on politics is Elvis's effect on pop music. When Elvis erupted on the scene, he was condemned as obscene, rude, and disruptive. The keepers of the gate suddenly became shrill and humorless: this perverse creature was ruining everything, and they kept talking about how it coarsened culture!

But they were right: after Elvis, pop music was *never* the same. Instead you got rock music. The Beatles. The Stones. Then you got psychedelic. Then you got heavy metal. Then punk. Then rap. And yes, dubstep polka. Like

Elvis, Trump just shattered a wall—but in politics. My prediction: you will see the same cascade of changes that you saw in pop music, but in politics, and you should be thrilled. Because it opens the political world up for something new, something fresh, something unpredictable. Trump will lead to Kanye, and Kanye will lead to God knows what. I can't even think of the next thing after President West. President Perino, if Dana isn't off running a resort for dogs.

The goal for Donald Trump mirrored his supporters—to upend the establishment, including the elites and the media that demeaned their beliefs and lives. But that profound accomplishment created an unbending mind in "the resistance"—a group of people who could not see any positive deeds in this administration, because their raw emotion clouded their ability to reason. And, also, because they lost.

THE CURSE OF THE SUNK COST

What contributes to an unbending mind?

It's the refusal to ever consider that your stance is wrong. "We were wrong" are the three little words that sociopaths never speak. Read the *New York Times* if you don't believe me. If you can never be wrong, then you can never allow a debate. Because at some point you will be hit with something that rocks your assumptions: and if you can't be wrong, then the only other alternative is punishment—demonization, career destruction, violence. The only plus to cure this mess is for the rest of us to *embrace being wrong.* To want to be wrong, at all times, allows you toward a path where you can then be right. I wrote an entire book on this. But I don't think it stuck.

I attribute this problem to something called "sunk costs," a financial term used to describe investments in something you don't ever get back. My life is punctuated by sunk costs. I once bought part of a dive bar. The fact that I had put money into it kept me attached to it, denying the evidence of this terrible decision that was staring at me right in my dumb face. Yes, employees and their friends were drinking for free; the neighbors hated us, and it was losing money like crazy. But that sunk cost kept me emotionally tied to this mess like a troubled ex. Until it closed. I never saw a dime of my investment, ever. I deserved it.

This happens with relationships, and with beliefs.

Recently I got a DM from "a friend of a friend." I had never met this person face-to-face, but we had chatted a few times online. After Trump's election, his missives had turned hostile, then vindictive. I won't say who he is, because really, I'd never even thought about him much. But apparently he had thought about me, a lot.

His first DM came shortly after the 2016 election. It asked me how I could live with myself, and how I could sleep at night, etc. I was confused by his anger (as I said, I've never met the guy), and so I asked him why. My mistake. He just unloaded on me.

This was my minus: to care. At all. In fact, I should make this paragraph shorter. (I just went back and cut out three sentences.)

But, this is a book, after all, so, instead of crapping on him, I laid down my weapons and explained my change of heart. I told him that I had once been angry about politics, and it was because I'd invested so much effort in one idea (beating Trump), without stepping outside my own cognitive cloud. It wasn't until Trump won that I decided to start over—give the new guy a chance, and shift to a more practical way of looking at life. (I decided to monitor Trump's deeds, and accept that his words are just words, and to quote the man himself, "See what happens.") Not only did my anxiety about politics lift, but I could think more clearly about the world in general. I could now talk to people whom I had earlier dismissed in their devotion to Trump. I could also see how my emotional response was simply that: emotional. Emotional! (Please scream this word out loud for effect.)

The guy told me to f*ck off. He could not abandon his sunk costs; the investment in past anger was too great. His hatred for Trump had carved a deep hole, so he couldn't climb out.

For many people—the longer you cling to an idea, the longer you must cling. Because, like all things in life, we invest in our willingness to stick around. We never say "I was wrong," because if we did, we'd never be able to say "I told you so." And we've also wasted so much time . . .

In such matters where you meet a mind like this, the other angry person personalizes the debate to such a point that what you say becomes a personal attack on them, and a moral judgment on you. All I was trying with the angry dude was to get him to admit that it's possible both of us could be wrong. After all, I have already done that for myself, and I felt great. Admitting being wrong is like getting a hit of a free, harmless, but fun drug. *It's a true plus, not a minus.* Letting go of your ego and admitting you're wrong feels almost as good as I imagine a nudist feels when he finally arrives at that secluded forest where he can throw his clothes into a pile and run into the brush, and get devoured by wolves.

The reluctance to admit you're wrong is due to time. Or rather investment. Time is not money; it's more than that.

Time is . . . time. You're on this planet for only so long, and when you put so much of it into something, it makes it that much harder to relinquish that commitment when it turns out you screwed up. You ever order a meal at a restaurant, and it's not what you expected, but you commit yourself to eating it, because, well—you paid for it? I never should order bat again (at least from a street vendor).

Anyone who has left a long relationship understands this. Women get it. The cliché about the clock ticking is rooted in reality, that is biology. True, we hold on to the long relationships because of the time invested, but women also have that extra layer of pressure: if you want to have kids, either freeze your eggs or get moving. It's the investment of time that keeps us locked in a bad scene. Because once you leave, where does all that time go? We see it as a waste, and we can't bear to think that everything we went through was for nothing.

But we've all done this, so that should be soothing in itself. So, why were you with someone when you knew it was going nowhere? If it had been three years, then that right there is your answer: it had been three years! How could you write that off? You feel like you can't so you go for five.

It happens with jobs, too. Did you stay at some place, because, well, you'd been there for so long? My example: working at *Prevention* magazine, and then *Men's Health*. I stayed there too long, because, well, I'd already stayed there too long. They had to fire me to get me out.

It's not about money, it's about time. Always. Which is why when you're at work, you should always be working, at something else. Like looking for another job. I'm personally taking a correspondence course in taxidermy right now. Who knows how long this TV thing will be around, and I do love a stiff ocelot.

Imagine doing anything for a long time with no payoff. Manhattan is littered with actors and actresses still clinging to the dream of stardom. And you can't tell them it's not happening. Their minds won't bend. Plus, you'll never get your entrée.

A bad idea clings harder than a fling who's nothing but trouble. If you ask yourself right now if you've ever been wrong about something in your life in the last year, and you can't think of one, then you're either lying to yourself or you're Jesse Watters. And I'm fairly certain you're not Jesse Watters. He's sitting across from me right now, coiffing his hair.

LEARN FROM YOUR AUDIENCE

The great thing about making mistakes is that if you make a lot of them, then you can give advice. You become an expert in fallibility! You're your own lab rat screwing up every maze. But hopefully you lived to talk about it afterward. The irony: Only make a few mistakes over a lifetime, and there's no book to write! Make a ton of errors and you can author a whole series!

(Yeah, yeah, I know, this is my ninth book. That joke writes itself.)

A few years ago, I was asked to speak at a conference in Florida. I had planned to speak for an hour before roughly six hundred people—like-minded souls: conservative, libertarian types who already knew who I was (the brilliant, leading man type from Fox News) and my sensibility (a cross between a court jester and a ferret). I figured it was a piece of cake. I was the first speaker that evening, during the dinner session; and as a special gift, I left a copy of my latest book on each chair, the cover featuring the likeness of yours truly. That stunt offered me a perfect opportunity to make what I thought would be a clever joke after my massive introduction applause died down. When the clapping stopped, I thanked the host, and said: "If you noticed before you took your seat—I left all of you a copy of my new book. I did that on the chance that half of you would end up sitting on my face."

I still think that was a pretty good joke, but of the six hundred or so people, I can safely say that maybe ten of them agreed. It's not that you could hear a pin drop after I said that.

You could actually hear a *shudder*. It was a good, clean lesson: whenever you walk into a room and make an ass of yourself, make sure you read it first. Works in city council meetings and in drunk tanks. My intro in Florida was a fail. And it would have been a bigger one, had the speaker following me not seemed completely unprepared (or maybe that's how I prefer to remember it).

A good thing: no matter how bad you may be doing, someplace on a planet with roughly 10 billion souls, somebody is probably doing worse. With luck, they're nearby, taking the heat off you. But the real lesson in failure was a boon for my future. It made me think about "the audience"—and to never take them for granted. It's an idea that I often scoffed at because I always believed that if I sprinted to some new, unique idea, it was up to the audience to keep up with me. I worked by this law in every job. It works until it doesn't; it's also obnoxious.

My job is predicated on not simply giving people what they want, but making it okay for them to want *me*. Every time you meet somebody new—or six hundred of them at once—there's always a good chance you'll get it wrong. Learn from my fail: my provocations can end up giving excuses to people on the fence to decide against me. I learned from then on that I had to be flexible, and get my ego out of the way, and make it easier for people to get me. Sometimes it's just better to not be totally you, all the time. (That's why sometimes I'm a young woman named Cassandra who lives in a trailer in Des Moines. I read palms and love pretzels!)

You have to be willing to bend, and change with the surroundings. Who you are at work may not fly at home, and vice versa. I find this out when I'm talking to my wife like she's a fellow panelist. She reminds me that we are not on TV and tells me to pick up my underwear.

I learned that even though I might be hired by a fan to do a speech, those people sitting out in that cavernous hall may have no idea what I do for a living (just like me, honestly). This is hard for me to value. I assume that being me is an effective, successful strategy—it's worked so far. But that's not always the case. My lesson: if you read the room, and it's not for you, *get the hell out.* But if you can't actually just leave, be willing to change. It's much better than insisting on being Captain Authentic. It's only one night.

I use this example because it's a lesson in inflexibility. The first step to real change is to be open to all kinds of change. Eliminate the frameworks that shape your destiny until you reach the limits of civility or legality. Because that destiny can end up as a joke that fizzles, at best. At worst, you can end up being insufferable around everyone. Think of all the successful people who should change because they won't read a room, and start with you.

THE PLUS

The Gumby Solution. How does an adaptable, flexible, easy-to-please kind of guy like you deal with an unbending mind? The first step is to recognize one early. If you can sense that there is absolutely no way in which to reach some understanding, with some difficult event or person in your daily life, probably the smartest thing to do is drop the attitude and back away slowly.

The minus here would be to engage aggressively, anticipating resistance or even conflict. The plus? To say, "Thanks for your time," and hail an Uber.

One plus you can try every morning is the "shoe on the other foot" trick. Once you examine how you feel about an issue, argue the opposite perspective. What you'll find is something akin to oppositional enlightenment—a phrase I coined just now, but feel free to drop it in conversation (no need to cite me). Whenever I do this, it only makes my argument stronger. And if it doesn't, then my argument might be wrong, or the issue might be super complicated.

Let's say you want to make an important point about an important issue. A plus is to not do it unrehearsed and in public. Meaning, if some friend on Twitter says, "I can't believe anyone could vote for Trump," the best way to respond is offline—so the effects of an audience do not degrade your behavior, or elevate the defenses of the other chap. It also helps in emails, to preface every point in which you're about to disagree with something like, "you may be right, but . . ." and never make an unambiguous statement without adding "IMO" at the end. "Aw, shucks" is better than shock and awe. I always dig a hole to climb out of with prefaces like, "Of course, what the hell do I know, but it seems to me . . ." I learned this from watching hundreds of *Columbo* episodes. The good lieutenant always solved the case, but along the way he played a dim bulb who, over time, grew brighter. My gut tells me that a lot of unbending minds are merely responses to other unbending minds. In fact, my own recent Gut-Lab study shows it takes only one muscle to say "no" but 640 to say "yes" (and 12 to say "dunno"). If you release an appeasement signal just by bending first, who knows what'll happen, especially in the shower.

Assess the real power, so you can give them some. When faced with an unbending mind, you're a hostage to their thinking. So the key is to indulge the hostage taker, so they'll be reminded that you're human. You're retraining them to communicate, but giving in a little to their irrationality. Cede some intel that might support their case—for it might open them up to listen to you. Think of it as a mental laxative for the intellectually rigid.

Write them off. It may be impossible to engage an unbender in conversation, which means making the mental note to never talk to this person about anything. Always have an out. There's one person I avoid, by always acting like I'm in the middle of an ongoing emergency. He may think that my life is a mess (someone's either sick or stranded), and feel bad for me—but because of that, he steers clear. It's a fair trade. I may only have three sisters but I have several dozen imaginary relatives who have broken everything from a timing belt to a clavicle.

Separate dislike from effects. When faced with a vociferous Never Trumper, the simplest strategy is to tell them that you're over their complaints—because their complaints are four years old (Trump's obnoxious, mean, scary, etc.). Ask them, "Do you have any new complaints that go beyond your issues with his personality?"

Then ask them who their favorite team is. Why is that important? Mine was the 1970s-era Oakland Raiders. I loved that team, even though Al Davis, the owner, had a reputation for being mercurial or brutal. His motto? "Just win, baby." In those three words, he managed to separate behavior from effects. Which is the first step for a Never Trumper to escape his mental emotional prison.

When the shark jumps, climb on its back. All good things come to an end, even that twelve-hour winning streak you call yesterday. Today may be much worse, and we always tend to see our unhappy present as the start of a miserable future. But days end, too, so one bad day doesn't mean a bad lifetime.

A bad day is like stepping onto one of those little spinning things they have in parks. Suddenly, everything's turning around you until you try to walk again and find yourself face-down in the sand pit.

There's bad news going on somewhere in the world (including in your cubicle, in your car, in your marriage, in your own life) every day, but resetting your compass won't help. It makes it worse. You still know the right way to go. Just face it: you won't get out of the swamp except by moving forward, slowly. So wait until the fascinating drama part of your bad day ends, eat something, snooze, and when the fog lifts, start again, carry on.

I know this is mind-numbingly simple, but it has the advantage of actually working. The rule of thumb plus: When you're in trouble, don't look back. Look forward. Replace dread with curiosity.

Imagine Dumping an Idea

Sunk costs based on past ideas are an emotional investment, just like anything else.

Look at ideas like investments. If it's looking bad, cut your losses. Don't feel any regret about changing your mind. Smart people dump bad ideas instead of clinging to them.

Now Try It on People

All relationships can be boiled down to one scary question. Is this person a plus or a minus in your life? The answer comes immediately. It's frightening, in fact, how fast the answer comes. How long it takes you to address the consequences of that answer is another problem entirely.

Then Try It on Your Job

If you hate your job, the job hates you back. We stay in jobs because leaving requires work. But if you use the negative space productively (like say, look for work while at your current place), a new opportunity might approach you without you ever leaving the building. This has happened at every single job I've had. I've never, ever left a company for a different one. You can get the new job, without the hassle. Until they ultimately fire you, which is what they did to me. And look at how that worked out!

Never Get Too Attached to Politics

Remind yourself that the impact of national politics is small compared to everything else in life (until they raise your taxes or legalize bestiality). More people watch your average NFL playoff game than any debate. Our government is constructed in a way so almost *nothing* happens (until it's too late). This notion will humble you when someone you actually like becomes president, and give you comfort when its someone you don't. Which is why Gumby always looked so happy—he could basically move in any direction, if persuaded. Also, he was buck naked (another key to happiness).

CHAPTER 4

THE PRISON OF TWO IDEAS

Most of my life, I thought that there were only two stances for every issue. I was either pro-this or anti-that. Made things simple and direct. But it was stupid and stifling. I call this problem "the prison of two ideas."

Below, I've made a list of things I've been wrong about, but initially thought I was right.

nuclear weapons will destroy the planet

nuclear weapons will save the planet

liberals are stupid, and worse, even dangerous

conservatives are intellectually superior

libertarians are annoying weirdos

libertarians have the right answer for everything

decriminalizing drugs is a bad idea

decriminalizing drugs is a good idea

Bernie Sanders is a dangerous lunatic

Bernie Sanders has some good ideas

climate change is a hoax

climate change isn't a hoax

I think I could lift a car off someone in an emergency

I think I have a heart condition

Trump is a harmful jackass who must be stopped

Trump might be the greatest president I've ever seen

the media sucks

the media sucks except for me

religion is for the fearful

no one has come up with anything better than religion

Buddhism seems pretty cool

Bruce Lee is really dead

Chevy Chase is a comic genius

Thor could beat Hulk even without his hammer

I am smarter than most people

I believed in most of those things because of that last point. I just assumed that intelligence was the main driver behind my decisions. Therefore, I was infallible. But the fact is, the smartest people on earth have been wrong about a lot of stuff. Look at George Will. Supersmart guy, but still dresses like a roadie for Devo. And he totally missed the boat on Trump, as did a lot of so-called experts the world over. The cautious ones said, "Never Trump!" and waited. The really mentally scarred ones left the GOP and voted for Hillary, which is like treating poison ivy by cutting off the infected arm. I got the election wrong, too—but at least I happily admit it on a daily basis. And by admitting my fallibility—hell, you can too!

The people who end up being right are the smart people humble enough to know when they're wrong. The people who do great on this planet are those who can see their mistakes and then share persuasively what the hell is really going on.

Churchill had his Gallipoli. Spielberg had *Hook*. And I had that interpretive dance phase. Let's just move on.

If you go over that list at the start of this chapter, you see that I must be wrong at least half the time. And that wrongness is due to what I call "the prison of two ideas." I either had to be pro-nuclear, or anti-nuclear; pro-drug or anti-drug, pro-Bernie or anti-Bernie. And so on. It's simplistic and stupid. For there is a range of beliefs that exists between those two rigid poles. And admitting that you're often wrong allows you to look at all those positions that exist in between. And that allows you to get closer to the truth. Which brings calm, happiness, and on occasion, free drinks.

Some people might call it "going soft," to abandon the strongest position for something more nuanced. But it's the opposite. Complexity is what life is—denying it only weakens your position. It's braver to leave the side of your pool and venture to the middle—even if it's just slightly over—to the other side.

I am convinced that if we were able to eliminate the prison of two ideas that guide lawmakers' decisions, we would all agree on exactly what to do with all our world's major problems—from homelessness to climate change to overweight adults wearing leggings instead of pants on plane flights.

Political obstacles, based on being imprisoned in two ideas, prevent us from solving even the most glaring problems. In today's *New York Post* (it's October 26, 2019, so technically today was a while ago) you'll find a perfect example: a story about a serial subway abuser who's been implicated, allegedly, in seven hundred crimes (!!!). He was just nabbed again for shoving a woman face-first into a stopped subway car—previously he'd been arrested for exposing himself. (Which is a very different thing. He's sort of the utility player of subway perps.)

Lawmakers repeatedly introduce laws to punish these maniacs—which get passed by the state senate with huge margins, only to die once they are put to a public vote in the assembly (I don't get it, either).

So if you ask anyone about this violent nut case, everyone with a reasonable brainpan would agree to put this psycho away for years. So why hasn't anyone done anything?

When interviewed anonymously, one assembly Democrat told the *Post* that it's liberal lawmakers who don't want to go on record in favor of "any tough-on-crime measures." They're afraid of going on record with a vote—and "if you had these bills voted on, and there was no record for who voted for what, I think you would see a dramatic difference in the laws in the state."

But because people in one party must publicly stay in its

own idea prison, they'd rather cast votes that end up allowing women to be assaulted in public places.

So a thug possesses an unlimited "get-out-of-jail-free" card, bestowed upon him by politicians who refuse to venture out of their self-contained prisons, for fear of being labeled bigoted by the media. He stays out of real jail, because they inhabit imaginary ones. "Irony" is one word for it. "Stupid" is another.

If there weren't these prisons of left and right, and a hyperactive, punitive media who castigates anyone who steps out of them, problems like maniacs on subways would be solved (as well as other problems like homelessness, mental illness, and drug addiction—which are all intertwined). But that first moment—when that one liberal Democrat considers actually voting for stiffer penalties for psychopaths—what does he fear? That a "woke" columnist will call him a fascist (after all, isn't the suspect the real victim!). That gets tweeted and activists will soon arrive to picket his office, with surprisingly uniformly printed signs. So rather than share that risk, he passes that risk off to female straphangers. They're on the front lines, not him—so he doesn't have to deal with the problem. But if we jettisoned these silly idea prisons, we'd be able to live better lives based on common sense. Sadly, current politics forces us into one of two positions, against the betterment of society.

Now, if you look at that list I casually tossed out, you'll see how I've changed my views often.

But now I pick views that range between two prisons, between two poles. I like to think I'm above it all, or maybe I'm just a man who likes stilts.

For instance, climate change isn't a hoax and we should pursue ways to protect the environment; but the conventional media has been plagued by faulty predictions and hysteria. Somewhere between hoax accusation and Greta Thunberg hysteria lies the truth: that even if the predictions are bad, we can work toward a cleaner environment—especially if we incorporate nuclear power (which is really the cleanest, most effective energy of all). As I put words to paper, President Trump just pledged to plant a trillion trees to reduce global CO_2 levels, at the same time condemning the prophets of doom saying the world will end in a decade. That, whether you want to admit it or not, is a stance that puts him outside both idea prisons. He's pivoted away from the "hoax" stance and walked outside toward practical action. But not without reminding us how hysteria works against actual progress.

Bernie isn't an idiot, even if he favors an idiotic ideology. He just favors the whole of something (socialism) when in fact part of his prescriptions can be useful in certain situations (a safety net—what kind of crazy Wallenda complains about that?). I just favor a vibrant free market economy that allows for a strong safety net that Bernie could never create in his failed socialist fantasies. Occupy Wall Street was an urban-camping farce that culminated in idiotic gestures, litter, noise, and crime. But since its implosion, I've met endearing minds who were part of it. They had legitimate beefs about Wall Street that were worth listening to, and maybe I should have listened more than condemned them (which I would have done if a few of their ugliest elements had not assaulted people). I still don't think Bernie has even two good ideas to rub together but I have to listen to him and respond, because dismissing him changes no minds at all.

Smart people can end up doing dumb things—watch me around last call—but writing them off entirely makes you a simplistic jerk. Bernie believes he's right—and I want to know how he can justify some of his beliefs that I believe have no evidence to support them. I think of them as helium-free trial balloons—colorful but going nowhere. So I'm still looking for Bernie's good idea. My guess is that he started with the goals first, and still hasn't figured out how to get there, besides confiscating wealth. And I don't like that, especially since he's had decades to figure it out, and hasn't. Joe Rogan just endorsed him (I am writing this in mid-January 2020) for being consistent. He's right: Bernie's been consistent . . . consistently wrong, like a stopped clock is consistently wrong. Throughout history he's backed the wrong horse from the luxury of a capitalist country where he can do that without ever happening upon a gulag.

But I can still like him. The way you like your quirky uncle who wears Kleenex boxes on his feet and never picks up a check.

As for the president, I've written about Trump before. When I had other options, I could easily dismiss his pro-wrestling demeanor (which makes me a hypocrite, I admit, since I'm no different at times, too). I also dismissed his supporters, some of whom were my friends and relatives. But when he won, I gave up my pet animus, and could see the appeal that I missed because I was toggling between other candidates.

Fact is, I thought what I was seeing in Trump was old news, but what his supporters were seeing was actually new. I was jaded by the glare of my own profession, while my friends and relatives, being normal Americans, were enamored. Ironically, the radical that the Left had dreamed of for America—their version of Che or Castro—actually *had* arrived. He was just a rich guy with wild orange hair in a baggy suit, instead of a rich guy in designer fatigues who could quote Howard Zinn.

And, of course, he was on the other side. The Left should

have seen that. But they didn't. And neither did I! And the persistent obstacle of Trump isn't what he's done so far, but what he's going to do next. Almost all the media is based on anxiety about the next horrible thing he will unleash. It never happens, of course; they're just selling ratings and newsstand copies. When you can't find what you want in reality, look to the future, where reality doesn't exist.

The main problem today? That the media rewards the two-prison framework, in full "makeup and hair," and sponsored by advertising. But they're just giving us what we want. We may claim we want nuance and subtlety—but I wonder how bored we'd be if someone tried to give it to us.

Imagine televised politics as any sport. There can only be two sides; there are no three-team basketball games. And it's not like you're going to give in to the other guy. It serves the networks ratings to find only two sides, and nothing in be-tween. Because one side feeds one audience and the other side feeds the other audience. But only allowing for two sides—a cemented framework found in all news—forces us to think we disagree about stuff we really don't disagree about. Once we let go of this structure, we see how easy it is to agree and move forward.

• • •

When I was an editor in my previous life, I was asked to discuss a story on a major network. Before the segment was to air, they did a pre-interview—asking me how I felt about some celebrity, and I gave them my perspective. They told me, sadly, that it was exactly the same as the person I was going to spar with, and it would be great if I'd take the other side. That pissed me off, that they assumed I could simply trade out an opinion just because—oh boy!—I would get to be on television! I should sell my soul for that spotlight. I refused to. And not simply because I'm a big hero, but because it was an early morning program, and I'd rather sleep in than sell my soul. (If it had been in the late afternoon . . . who knows?) And my soul's not worth that much anyway. I put it on eBay for $32.99. No takers.

Thing is, this producer was just doing her job. And her job was delivering debate to an audience that craves it. She was right: people come to TV for disagreements, as long as their side clobbers the other. It's pro wrestling with inferior costuming and less humor and hair. The fire of a distant debate beats the cozy sweater of agreement. Everyone on the same page? That's boring. That's a panel on CNN debating something they all agree on, like the evils of memes that make fun of CNN. Boring. And what else is boring? Nuance, complexity, *footnotes*. Plus, such things take up a lot of time. If you've got four minutes for a segment on an average program and the host asks me about my stance on immigration and I respond with "I am for the lottery system, against the skilled worker visa, and we should build a wall while simultaneously increasing the numbers of refugees, provided they take a course in capitalism," I guarantee I will never be asked to return. Yet, that's pretty much my stance, I think. For now, anyway. It could change.

There are true polarities in this world. In the digital world there are ones and zeroes, and in life there is life and death, rich and poor, ugly and me. But there's a load of upholstery in between that can make your life easier. Take foreign policy. We used to think of it as only war and peace. Tolstoy never wrote *War and Extended Cease-fire Talks* because he knew nobody would read it. Which is a problem—because with the war-peace dichotomy you've got a 50 percent chance you're going to lose a nephew, a son, daughter, or dad.

But soon you realize that diplomacy is nothing more than an endless series of little steps, boring meetings that are placed between the polarities of "doing nothing" and "killing everyone." An example: sanctions, which are the financial penalties enacted against a country that's pissed you off.

Did you ever notice how there's always one more sanction to apply after the previous sanction? Each new sanction seems always to be more severe than the one before it, until you're finally sanctioning cuff links and novelty ashtrays. There never seems to be a final sanction—just another harsher, more desperate one that features tariffs, restrictions on financial dealings, and trade barriers. I feel like sanctions are always available and made to order, like an omelet station at a really boring buffet.

Yet, what do you see these days on cable and social media? Orchestrated polarizations. Men vs. women. Blacks vs. whites. Rich vs. poor. You don't see community anymore—you see A vs. B. If you hate vowels, you know which side you're on.

What you get from that is the death of real conversation. Of debate. Instead, everything becomes a fight—and these days, it's often personal. In that case, supporting Trump, for example, is akin to being a storm trooper, a Nazi, a concentration camp guard. That's where the prison of two ideas takes you. You have to keep getting more and more extreme, until you're treading air like Wile E. Coyote. And how can you talk about anything if the person you're talking to sees anything you say as an attack on their own "identity"? Instead, you just shut up. Believe me, I've been there.

You'll be in a debate, and the other person will pause. Her voice softens just slightly as she shifts to a personal story. Because sentiment sells and sense doesn't, this will only be encouraged. And even though emotion is normal, it's becoming the replacement for actual thoughts. Take climate change: the personalization can come down to: "this is my planet—and you're evil for polluting it and killing my kids." That's now how CNN looks at science. Or take snack foods (hash browns or fries?) or haircuts (a fade or a flop?) or losers (the Mets in 1962 or Hillary in 2016?). All of these ultimately are driven by emotional investment. Psychologist Jordan Peterson claims that when two men argue there's always the understanding that it can end in a fight. It's why I never argue with myself.

If you look hard enough, you can personalize every issue. Is it worth it? You have to ask because once it's personalized, it kills debate. It becomes one person's truth, instead of something you can rationally talk about. It creates one prison in the two-prison universe of ideas, where only a pure stance must exist, and anything that deviates is a personal attack. Normally, in a debate, "nothing's personal." No more. The personalization of debate deems any kind of hard truth harmful to one's fragile health and eliminates any chance for real conversation. And, as Peterson suggests, it ends in a punch or a call to 911 or both. The stakes for any argument are ridiculously high.

Perhaps that's the whole point.

THE PLUS

How to add legs to your two-legged stool. Only journalists love binary thinking. That's why poll responses that include "none of the above" and "no opinion" are despised—they get in the way of a story so simple even a journalist can understand it. It's the "except in the case of" responses that open the door to complications, and that means research and that means work and that's the edge of the media's flat earth.

Your friends in the press love unbalanced political situations. Think of a stool with only two legs: Will we lean left? Right? Elites say "Left!" while the independents say "Right!" The hearings are at a deadlock. The decision could go either way. The result is always too close to call. Oh, and, uh, don't miss the news at ten! No wonder anxiety is the cash crop of the media business.

Why live your life that way? When you don't know which way to go, try straight ahead and down the middle. Commit to compromise. Allow for exceptions.

Find the Wave and Surf It

The fact is, everything, including breathing, where every inhale demands an equal and opposite exhale, boils down to a choice between two opposites:

Reading/not reading this book.

Moving/not moving.

Sending me a hundred dollars/sending me only fifty.

We refer to computers as digital for one simple reason: they're made of units called bits that are either "on" or "off." (There, you just got a degree from Gutfeld University in computer science. We also offer animal husbandry.) And if our existence is actually a simulation, as many mad scientists now believe (the simulation hypothesis suggests that all reality is in fact artificially simulated—likely designed via computer; it's the egghead version of religion) what does that mean? Well, it means that our very existence is, at its core, a choice between on and off. Is it a wonder that almost everything we do can be boiled down to two choices, when that's what we are literally made of? Yes or no? Now or then? On or off? Dead or Alive. (They had one great hit, remember? "You Spin Me Round.") Pete Burns, we miss you.

In science, there is something called "wave-particle duality." I won't pretend to understand quantum physics—or even biophysical or electromagnetic physics—but the concept provides a direction to enhanced thinking: the wave-particle duality says that every particle may be described as either a particle or a wave. This helps describe the concept that a particle can be in more than one place at the same time. I don't want to lose you (I see you, Tom Stevens, putting this book down in your Omaha living room to go make a sandwich), but in short: once you measure the position of a particle, the particle has changed position—making the position of said particle always an uncertainty (until it's measured). Proving once and for all that physicists don't need drugs.

But the explanation of wave-particle duality makes actual sense when you apply it to ideas and arguments.

Right now you're in that dual prison, where each position on an issue is seen as fixed—a particle in space. When in Gutfeld's reality, a position is a wave—a series of endless and uncertain positions that come into being the moment one wishes to measure it. Once you begin thinking this way, it expands your thinking, and allows for clever and surprising directions for your thoughts. And even more, when more people do this, the chance for overlap—meaning when your idea and their idea share the same wave—becomes much more likely.

Repeat after me: your argument isn't a particle, it's a wave. Dude. Now see where that wave takes you.

Note: this doesn't mean that morality is subjective. This isn't a way of escaping judgment for bad crap, and saying "murder isn't really murder!" I'm talking about seeing what else is out there beyond a fixed stance. For example: a total ban of illicit drugs is a prison. Total legalization is also a prison. Somewhere in between is what humans want, because they attenuate the challenges of life. Also, it's fun.

THE SHOE ON THE OTHER FOOT, REALIZED.

Here's a Plus moment about the time I pushed the crème pie of hypocrisy into my face.

Usually incidents that reveal your own contradictions in thought and action happen too far apart to enable some kind of connective intellectual tissue.

For example: you're driving to work one day, and you shake your fist at a careless jaywalker lost in the noise from his headphones.

A week later, you're jaywalking, listening to your favorite Norwegian death metal, and you smirk at the oncoming driver who must slow down because unlike you he values human life.

We often don't see these things side to side: if we did, we'd forever change our behavior.

Or go nuts.

But it happened to me recently. And it revealed to me a larger observation than the simple "We're all hypocrites" and narrowed it down to "I am a hypocrite."

What we see in others, for some reason, we cannot see in ourselves.

I don't know why, but maybe when I'm done writing this, I will.

Here's the story: At work we had a scheduled photo shoot for a show, and as usual, I'm a pain in the ass. I hate photo shoots, with impatient strangers pleading with you to smile and all that. I complained about it for weeks, until the day of the shoot. And on that morning, I got extremely physically ill. I called in sick. So I didn't go.

Instead, I had to go to doctors, then the hospital, and undergo a litany of tests.

Because I missed the photo shoot, it created a problem for the other participants, who had all shown up in spite of whatever obligations they had elsewhere. The shoot was scrapped. There was a palpable sense of disgust directed at me, and for obvious reasons: they didn't believe I was sick. They thought I had just played hooky (is that still a word?). After all, I had been complaining for weeks—and then coincidentally, I just didn't show up? Please.

I was mad that people questioned my excuse. I ended up getting numerous MRIs and scans, so how dare they make light of such things! (It turns out I have a very unusual disorder that only tertiary characters in soap operas get—I'll tell you about it on the book tour if you ask, or if it turns out to be contagious.)

Fast-forward a month. I'm supposed to have a meeting with someone at work who I know doesn't really want the meeting and has been complaining about it for a while.

And sure enough, the day before the meeting, he says he's ill. He can't come in.

I didn't buy it. I complained to my friends. I said it was total obvious bullshit.

Then of course, three days later, he's going into surgery. I felt awful, but obviously not as awful as he felt.

Maybe because these two events happened one after another, I could see how easily I had switched sides. But could I see the mechanism that allows you to do that? How could I rip my coworkers for the instincts they had about me, when I had the same instincts about one of them just a few weeks later?

It's a curse of being your own first person. You're the storyteller and the narrator of your life. You portray your life the way you want it to be seen. Plus, you have no editor crossing out the bad stuff. So it's just you covering up the flaws in you that you point out in others.

I find that I am most critical of others' shortcomings if they are similar to mine. It's probably why I am terrified of having kids. When I see coworkers (those younger than me) who share my talents and therefore my flaws, I am more harsh on them than on others. It's pure transference: when I see you make my mistakes, I'm taking it out on you—for the both of us.

So. How do you know when you're doing unto others what you don't want done to you?

It's a very simple Plus test: Pretend you're them. Put that shoe on the other foot—and I don't mean put your left shoe on your right foot. I mean, stand in somebody else's place and see how it feels. Or pretend you're their lawyer, and in your head, argue on their behalf. It might not change your behavior, but it might reveal the cognitive weirdness of perspective. It's the truth of the perfect mirror—one step closer to wisdom and one step away from being a jerk.

Embrace Infinity

One day when I was *definitely not high*, I started thinking about something called Zeno's paradox. According to my friend Wally Wikipedia, in its simplest form, Zeno's Paradox says that two objects can never touch. The idea is that if one object (say a ball) is stationary and the other is approaching it, the moving ball always passes a halfway point before reaching the stationary ball. In other words, any distance or amount can always be split in half. You can see why his friends would never lend this Zeno guy any money.

That means almost nothing to me, especially while trying to uncork a bottle of wine without an opener, until I read an explanation that is perhaps better, from a popular math book by some guy whose name escapes me. He explains the same theory that basically there's an infinite series of numbers in between two numbers.

So I'll translate: Let's say you're at the Marriott Express in Midland, Texas, and you're walking from your hotel (room 100) to your manager's room, which has the bourbon (room 101). There's a halfway point between the rooms. When you get to that halfway point, you end up with a new halfway point between your current location and room 101. When you reach that next halfway point, the division continues. Even when you're basically standing in front of room 101, there still is a tiny halfway point between the toe of your shoe and the door. And, yes, there's a halfway point beyond that—and so on and so on until your head explodes. There are basically infinite halfway points—or in my translation: infinite positions you can take in life. There aren't two positions, there are a zillion. Don't let anyone tell you differently. Especially any guy named Zeno—he's probably an imposter, since the real guy's been dead a few years.

Crap, maybe I was high when I theorized this. So was Zeno, likely. But here's the plus: instead of hotel rooms 100 and 101, look at them as simply two positions on an issue. And between those two positions (rooms, or prison cells if you will) there are an infinite number of places to go. You shouldn't feel pressured to adhere to either one. Just do what I did and pass out on the hallway carpet. (Those Marriott housekeepers are a grumpy lot.)

I can tell you that the smartest people I know navigate in that infinite space. These are the people who surprise you—holding a position on limiting immigration in one category, while pushing for unlimited immigration in another. You can be pro on one part, and against on another. The best minds on the planet—from Penn Jillette to Scott Adams to Bret and Eric Weinstein to Robert Wright and Dave Rubin—create their own positions, refusing to be placed in what others think is right. Eric Weinstein, in particular, has a brilliant way of looking at issues. Boiled down: you can hold ideas the way you hold investments. There are long position and short positions on everything, simply by looking at the "relative value" investment. I'd give an example, but my head hurts thinking about it. Ask him, he'll explain it.

If I remember this correctly, Zeno was a Greek philosopher born half a millennium before Christ, and who spent most of his time pondering infinity. Since there is an infinity of terms in that progression, this dead Greek guy will never reach Point B, which I hope doesn't stand for bathroom, because he'll never get there in time, and then the housekeeper will be really pissed.

And in that fable lies a measure of happiness. Instead of being stuck between two poles—a prison of ideas—you have an infinity of options to choose from. You don't have to be pro or con on anything; instead you can move a little this way, or a little that way—and eternally confound TV producers everywhere. It's true, you will not get a hosting gig on *The Daily Outrage*, but you'll probably end up being the smartest person in the room, which is easy if the room is at Columbia's Journalism School.

CHAPTER 5

HOW TO CANCEL "CANCEL CULTURE"

We've been lunching on a lie since high school.

The lie was this: those wishing to take away your freedom would come in the form of some massive monolithic, soulless government. We had to worry about faceless bureaucrats and faceless, armed mobs with mysterious insignias busting our doors in the dead of night, scooping us out of our beds, where we're vanned to reeducation camps somewhere underground, a place with no internet, no cable, no sushi—not unlike certain parts of New Jersey. Which would be fine with me, because I hate sushi. But the "no internet thing" would be a problem. Because I love cat videos.

What bullshit. At least in America. We've solved the oppressive-government thing long ago. Which now means that the attacks are not coming from above us, but from below and basically from everyone around you. It's not the government that is Big Brother, it's *us*.

Cancel culture is a lame phrase, but so what—that's what we're talking about. It's a form of public shaming aimed at destroying people's lives under the guise of "holding them responsible for their actions." It can and has resulted in rabid Twitter mobs, boycotts, and public figures being showered with milk shakes (if they're lucky, it's *only* milk shakes), and even violence against speakers on campus. Because it's driven by an imagined moral imperative it makes violence "okay," hence antifa mobs who think they're doing history a favor when they beat up a stranger with a bike lock.

If you're to ask a public shamer why they're targeting someone, they'll almost always say, "because this person's behavior is problematic." That word—problematic—acts as a massive blanket that covers any or all behavior activists don't like, but can't explain why without meaningless buzzword salads. The usual targets for canceling can be celebrities, but it can also be anyone with an unpopular opinion, or something in their past that doesn't hold up to present-day morality. Of course, what is problematic they also deem as evil.

Cancel culture seems to be what you get when you finally have almost everything. All the big problems are on their way to being solved: so let's turn on each other. We have no Nazis—now we have fourteen or so sort-of Nazis—and a complex of media, academia, and entertainment industries telling us where to point our weapons: at the oppressors among us. Which ultimately, becomes all of us. It turns out we're surrounded by Big Brothers.

It's something we all understand these days, but are scared to discuss: this ever-expanding and somewhat arbitrary witch hunt. Because, after all, we are afraid to discuss *anything*, period. What if we speak out? What if we share a little bit of risk? Then the glaring light moves toward us. Then we become the hunted.

We are afraid to talk, to joke, to vent, to express an opinion in general, because who knows who or what might be lurking around the corner, with a smartphone and a score to settle? We used to call them finks, hall monitors, tattletales. Not any more. Now they are analysts! Journalists! Whistle-blowers with lawyers! Speakers of truth to power! On CNN, they call them "reliable sources."

Thanks to a consensus corporatist media driven by profit and division, and a restless bored public that flocks to any fireball controversy, our nation is now overrun with hysterical narcs there to feed an ambivalent populace. A small but intense group of people are dying to nail you on something (historically, a cross), as the larger but fearful crowd who won't step in to protect you sits back and watches, praying that they aren't next.

Last fall, I watched a comedian I had never heard of get fired from *Saturday Night Live* for some old racist jokes he tweeted before he even started the job. Oddly, only a handful of comedians came to his defense, likely because they feared that by doing so, the spotlight might shift to them, and their own mildly linguistically reckless, sullied past. In this era, the canceling of careers by nobodies with no skin in the game has turned into a giant game of Whac-A-Mole, so the natural instinct is to keep your head totally underground—even if it means biting your lip when one of your friends gets caught in that imaginary net.

The creature we fear is no longer the mysterious "them." It's us, our worst selves. The shrill and angry vessels of boredom who lurk among us. We can say what obviously fuels the division—in fact, I always do. it's social media. Nothing generates more clicks and attracts more feverish attention than a feeding frenzy around a person who might have violated an invisible, unwritten, always-changing code. And God help you if you're the wildebeest separated from the herd. The Twitter hyenas will be on you like it's their last day at the water hole. It's also a self-perpetuating machine: if the media sees a story in which five people comment on the mistakes of another, to them, that's a story. Here's the synopsis:

1. Joe Thompson says something slightly un-PC while doing the local weather report in Catasauqua, Pennsylvania.

2. Someone, usually a poorly paid blogger for some massive media outlet, posts it. He's a lowly writer with no experience, so he slams Joe hard, not even bothering with a reporter-ly phone call.

3. Twitter erupts! (Meaning lonely people tweet "I'm shaking as I read this . . . ") That poorly paid blogger ends up, briefly, a star among his circle of other lowly hacks.

4. Joe is trending on Twitter, which causes another blogger, this time for CNN—which writes its default headline featuring two key words: "sparks" and "outrage." When something "sparks outrage," you don't need a who, a where, a when, a what, or a why. It's a sentence in which the object becomes the subject (try to diagram that one).

To prove this is an actual story, said blogger says, "Here are 4 responses by people with blue check marks next to their names!" One is probably a sputtering d-bag Patton Oswalt. In the era of Twitter, what constitutes a story is now based on what "some say"—the kind of story that gets retweeted again and again, until it's no longer just four people who are upset, but "many," four hundred, which in the twittersphere can feel like four million . . . especially if you're that poor guy named Joe. And those first four people who make up that total "twitterstorm" of the truly outraged takes a victory lap. We got a scalp! What do we do now?

At some point, to save his job, the poor weatherman (or whoever he was: frankly I forgot already) decides he must offer a groveling apology, but he still gets fired. He's canceled. He ends up living in his parents' attic, wondering if he should change his name to something less attention-getting, like "Ted Bundy."

It's happening not just to the well-known, but even to the obscure, including someone just trying to do good. As I write this, some college kid managed to raise a few bucks by asking for free beer on TV during a football game (I'm actually amazed no one thought of this sooner). Corporate sponsors piled on. Soon he had millions! So he gave it all to a children's hospital. I know: what a monumental asshole!!!

So, what did the media focus on? Well, some reporter sifted through a boatload of tweets and posts and rewarded himself with a big scoop when he found out that when the college kid was a teen, he posted a few crappy "problematic" tweets. The reporter could smell the Pulitzer (it was probably just body odor).

Suddenly, instead of the guy's amazing charitable achievement, the big story became his racist past. It's true, something dumb posted four years ago outweighs raising millions for kids with cancer.

Ironically, the reporter who scored this amazing scoop was then fired when his earlier "problematic" tweets were uncovered—which I also find "problematic," or hilarious! The children's hospital still got the money, but not without our scandal-craven media extracting some pain from the guy who raised it—possibly scaring anyone else from repeating the same good deed. I know I won't be raising any money for a children's hospital today! (Scratch that off my to-do list.)

The cancellation of careers isn't just some weird phenomenon you can blame on the rise of Twitter and Facebook alone (though they're certainly accomplices). It's bigger, and possibly darker, than that. Imagine Pontius Pilate's Twitter feed. Social media is just the funnel for a new kind of political action—one that harnesses hysteria, envy, and restless anger, adorned with convenience and ease-of-use. It's not just to disagree with ideological opponents, but to wipe out, eradicate, and cancel people whose views are different, or whose personalities simply don't fit. We are targeting not just the controversial for extinction, but the obnoxious as well.

When Joe Rogan—a good stoned liberal—endorsed ultra-lefty Bernie Sanders, what happened to him? People *to the left* of Bernie (if that is indeed possible) outed Rogan as a racist bigoted transphobe. The cancel culture was set in motion. Rather than argue why his endorsement might be wrong—or "problematic"!—they decided to cancel the imaginary Nazi making the endorsement. Lucky Rogan has a big enough following to prevent this from ruining his insane career. But I hope this experience opens Joe's eyes even more to this toxin—one that, sorry, Joe—was exacerbated by leftists like . . . Bernie Sanders!

Cancel culture loves to nail people for stuff they said . . . or hell, stuff someone else said! Just ask NASCAR driver Conor Daly, who lost a major team sponsor after his dad admitted to using a racial slur three decades ago. It's tertiary transmission of offensiveness! (This might be one other excuse for me not to have children: Why put them through the hell of wondering when my words will come back to haunt them? I've said enough things to scar generations.)

Here's a scary thought. What if the society (a free-market capitalist America) that came up with most of the solutions for the world's most pressing problems is on its way out? What if having people target each other online for career extinction and humiliation could be the best way to bring down a society, and without ever having to lift a weapon? What if achievement and inventiveness aren't worth the risk? Remember, a few years ago, that guy who landed a spacecraft on a comet? Matt Taylor was the British scientist who safely dropped a module on a comet some 300 million miles away, a feat that no one has ever done, ever. But after the landing, on camera, Taylor made the mistake of wearing a shirt with cartoons of scantily clad women holding firearms. He was swarmed on Twitter, mocked all over the internet, until he apologized in tears. It was cancel culture at its finest. I wonder if landing a module on a comet will be his *last* achievement, precisely because the spotlight isn't worth another one.

What if the folks who deemed America's system hopelessly oppressive suddenly realized that, instead of violent revolution (which would go nowhere—thank you, Second Amendment and my purple belt in karate), they could just uproot society by simply demolishing civility and trust?

You can't have one without the other. So if you can't organize a coup, why not just galvanize a social media mob to tear each other apart? Isn't that what Jussie Smollett (a TV actor, I'm told) tried to do? His alleged hoax had the power to spark a race war. Thankfully, it was too hilariously absurd to be taken seriously, although the other usual media suspects had immediately swaddled the creep in sympathy (while the rest of us quietly puked).

I know this theory sounds nuts, but isn't that what we're doing now to just about anyone whose achievements puts them in the crosshairs of our ravenous media? We are killing achievement, because the possibility of going far and doing good brings the media glare that exposes the mistakes of your past.

This stuff actually doesn't need a dark purpose to explain its existence. It's just an easy thing to do for dumb people. If I can't respond to a person's arguments with ones of my own—why not just label that jerk a racist? If I still cannot fathom how President Trump won, or how he was able to resonate with so many people, can't I just say that they're all misogynistic bigots? And similarly, rather than consider thoughtfully Bernie Sanders' connection with voters, can't I just call them commie fascists?

That's kind of where we are, no? (Don't answer that—if I'm wrong then I have to rewrite the book.)

A lot of this stuff is done casually. Meaning, that after we ruin lives, we just move on, forgetting the permanent impact we left on some shell-shocked stranger. It's like the old lady who ran over your bicycle when you were twelve and just kept going (talking about you, Mrs. Gladwell, and your Dodge Dart). That's how it works in an ambivalent, affluent society, enjoying endless leisure time and swollen IRAs. The kids of well-off parents, bored and dulled by easy pleasure, find that hit of dopamine every time they cancel a nobody or, better, a non-nobody on Twitter.

It's entirely possible that the misery junkies fueling cancel culture are doing it because they have nothing else going on in their lives. And that "nothing else" could be beyond their control—consequences of a society that paradoxically offers dwindling opportunities for fulfillment despite offering huge opportunities for distraction.

We've essentially killed off religion. Even as an agnostic, I see harm in this. It creates a nation of wanderers, nuts, and angry misfits. When you look at cancel culture—what could be the natural solution? "Love the sinner, hate the sin" is a good place to start—in any disagreement. But we threw that baby out with the bathwater. Now the sinner *is* the sin—as mobs damn the sinner to everlasting hell. We could use a savior right about now. Or maybe admit to ourselves that religion got a few things very right, even if that upsets your edgy atheist friends.

We all engage in behaviors we hate. Perhaps that's why we hate those behaviors so much. We look at them—the shaming, gossip, mobbing—and we see ourselves in them. I know I see myself in these things, and I wish I didn't.

So I hate social media, because I use social media. I am social media. I despise Twitter, but I am on it. My name is Greg, and I tweet. Okay? I'm on a twelve-step that will probably land me on Instagram. I can't stop looking. I see one crash after another. It's like living in the median stop on the New Jersey Turnpike waiting for a really good head-on. Giving camera-cool smartphones to the general public is like turning everyone who has ever felt even a slight surge of anger into their own TMZ. You look at the guy who cut you off, then at the device in your hand and think "Hmmm, what can I do with this?"

In the online battlefield, the machinery of the media mob targets, mobilizes, and liquidates. And because no one has the courage for empathy, there can be no potential for redemption. Once you are canceled, you are canceled, for good. You cannot leave your house, unless in disguise. You must remove yourself from all social media. You may not get any more work, if your work was once in the public arena. If you once were a writer or a speaker, you shall be permanently scrapped. You cannot come back. You are done. And if you try to come back, someone in the media universe will be waiting to stomp on you again. If you think your former friends will step up to save you, you're looking under the wrong rock.

It is now recreational sport to destroy each other, then quickly move on to new and vulnerable prey. This is a new world, friends. It's a new world where:

- you define a person's intent at its very worst. Why waste perfectly good faith when you may need it yourself? If a joke by someone isn't just a joke, but evidence of darker, hateful intent (racist, sexist, anything that ends in *-ist*), score one for you and your virtue. You're one step closer to internet fame.

- apologies become tantalizing chum to your adversaries. Even a mild apology tells them a victory is in sight and therefore your sad, little expression of "regret" will mean little in terms of actual sincerity to those who hear it. If you want to sincerely apologize, cut off your leg with a chain saw. Otherwise, an apology only encourages others to pile on.

- the distant, careless past is always present, and can never be excused: a tweet from five or ten years ago defines who you are today, and one can never scrub that stain off your soul. You can never recover—social media humiliation is also a career-death penalty. These sad people who "mine" for old tweets actually exist. Once someone is in the news

(Kevin Hart is named an Oscar host, briefly, for example), the Twitter mining crew springs into action! (Career-boosting tip for eager tweet-mining "journalists" looking for dirt: for the best stuff, look for tweets posted before March 21, 2006.) And forget revenge. These tweet-miner's lives are so insignificant that the target for reciprocity is too small.

- As part of social media's redefinition of its role, the old guard media are now national hall monitors, seeking violations of present-day rules to exact wrath. Remember when CNN tracked down the nobody behind a GIF that had Trump wrestling a character with the CNN logo as its head? They scared the crap out of him enough to cause him to publicly apologize (note: it was the media who intimidated him, not a government or militia). Then there's that same network's "special investigation" in which a reporter harasses some older Florida woman for being "influenced by Kremlin-linked trolls" on social media.

Did you think for a moment that this massive media machine might realize that they might be punching down when they went after some frightened old lady? Or maybe when you're as low as the CNN crew in their little clown cars, you can't get low enough to actually punch down. So CNN sends out a front-end loader to swat fleas. Fleas may be small, but they're bigger and braver than CNN. Fleas have higher jumps in their ratings, too.

Scapegoating (singling out a person or group for unmerited blame) has become a job for losers out to even the score (see Media Matters), quenching their own desire for achievement by denying the success of others.

Companies, peer groups, and even friends will distance themselves from you once you land in hot water, rather than boldly sharing the risk against a small group of scalp hunters. Such behavior incites paranoia, as people rush to protect themselves.

Companies, especially, have no idea how to deal with any angry Twitter mob—even if the mob is one person and their pet canary. And because of that, they cannot comprehend a real threat when it reaches one of their employees. If some weirdo flips out on Twitter, it may feel like a crowd of thousands.

And it works! It takes as few as just three angry trolls to instill the fear of a "backlash" against almost anything, turning irrational fears of boycotts into absolute realities. This is because human resource departments, which is where corporate morality hides itself, would rather cower than stand up for their employees, or even their own products. Not long ago,

Gillette jumped on the misandrists' anti–"toxic masculinity" bandwagon—until a genius in advertising realized they were condemning their customer base. You remember: the ad had a bunch of scenes where overly masculine men bully women, and the actions naturally dismissed as "boys will be boys." It was exactly how an ad might be written by a nervous guy trying to stay in the good graces of a Twitter mob. Makes sense—after all, there aren't enough gender studies professorships available, so logic holds some of them would end up in the workforce, where they can do real damage.

We've all seen successful campaigns that force colleges to ban speakers, to divest from companies, to condemn whole countries, to ban courses and the professors who had the gall to offer them. Now activists target corporations with the same tactic. And it's working. On campus they politicize investments (in Israel, especially, since that's the "acceptable" anti-Semitism), sponsors, and advertisers. If activists hate your opinion, they won't debate you, they'll just target the people who pay you. But it really isn't about being upset over an idea: it's having power over you. And corporations are run by a fearful sort of person—as crisis management expert Eric Dezenhall told me, the myth of the ruthless corporation is just a myth. They're so risk-averse, they'll give in at the sight of single retweet of a negative tweet. And the social media mob, which is fed by the larger, moralizing media, knows that today companies bend like yoga instructors in a tornado, rather than gauge the actual effect of the paltry mob.

The response to this weaponized, targeted activism is a phony veneer of fatuous virtue-signaling with stupid sanctimonious tweets about whatever cause is the cool thing that month. This works, at least temporarily. But virtue-signaling is just a chicken disguising itself as a bush, hoping the fox walks past him. It works for a few minutes, until you say, "Cluck!" Then it's over.

This new environment of canceling creates suspicion even among coworkers and friends. It's like the old Soviet Union: you don't have to surveil everyone, just make sure everyone thinks they're being surveilled. And that'll get the citizens to report on one another, to do their job for them.

So, if we now get the vibe that we are all under the watchful gaze of Big Brother, what happens to our daily work and social life? It's reduced to a more platonic version of an Amish couple at a drive-in.

These days, you cannot hold a meeting with anyone without the suspicion that they might be recording it or hold a meeting with anyone privately without having a third person present just as an insurance policy against accusation. Comedians now force fans to sign NDAs at shows, and now many entertainers force concertgoers to dump their phones in those special "Yondr" pouches (which sounds like something a prospector kept his toilet paper in).

So once a victim is targeted and then eradicated, there is no road back for them—no apology is enough; therefore, redemption is ridiculous; forgiveness is forever banned. Instead of seeking a better gig, you might resign yourself to be happy with the one you have. Because success brings a spotlight. Scalping kills ambition better than a hydroponic weed habit and unlimited Netflix.

And because there is such a low entry cost for taking part in social media, scapegoating always encourages new, hungry players who are quickly rewarded. You may be a loser in real life, but on Twitter, you can easily make an impact. You can cost a man or woman his or her job, family, happiness. That is more power than a cellar-dwelling loser ever had in his or her life. You go from Willy Loman to Thanos.

So what is the end result? Since actual success is rewarded with humiliation, maybe it's better to lie low, and achieve little, than make a name for yourself and attract the vultures of success.

In an increasingly technology-dependent world, we are told machines will take over many of our jobs. But the jobs they can never master should be the ones that rely on empathy and communication.

But what happens if we already decided that we can't handle those aspects of humanity anymore? What happens if we make communication and empathy unacceptable? If one side deems the other side not just wrong but *evil*, then conversation is pointless, and empathy becomes impossible.

We end up doing the robots' jobs for us. We kill our own humanity, before they have a chance to do it for us. We sit here and fret over artificial intelligence and killer bots, but they'll never come close to the havoc humans wreak on each other.

And the people leading the charge—the media titans and the social media titans—are so blinded by their bias, they don't see that their idiocy makes them equally vulnerable. To hoaxes, especially.

THE HOAXES BEHIND THE HATE

Within cancel culture, the life creates its own punishments, but also its own rewards. We are incentivizing victimhood—and creating a new kind of theatrical stab for recognition.

Right now, according the people tabulating this stuff

(known as actuaries, or more accurately, number-weenies), we're experiencing a perceived rise not in actual hate crimes, but in hate crime hoaxes. I say "perceived" because the numbers admittedly are spotty.

The media would have you believe we have a huge rise in hate crimes, but upon a closer look, it's not so much.

Wilfred Riley, assistant professor of political sciences in the College of Public Service and Leadership Studies at Kentucky State University, may have a name out of a 1950s sitcom, but he's one of the few people I've found who's looked at this closely enough. His research of hate-crime allegations by around four hundred or so people showed that fewer than a third could be called "genuine hate crimes," a definition only requiring that it wasn't a "crime" exposed as a hoax, or not discovered to have been perpetrated by a person different from the originally accused.

What purposes do hoaxes serve, besides attracting attention to the perp? They exist to sustain the activist's crusade, to help them prove themselves right. No cause or campaign raises money by saying, "Hey, things are getting better!" And as long as you create the illusion that healing is impossible, then the attention you receive will never end. You're set. The media will climb all over each other to get you on their shows. Of course, until the hate crime is exposed by some scrappy skeptic, who pulls at one thread from that suspicious sweater, which begins the unraveling. (That's what happened with Jussie Smollett: it was the persistent work of local Chicago journalists who refused to bend to the national media's need for a momentous hate crime that would define the Trump era. And I bet those gutsy reporters weren't even Trump voters.)

And that's usually when the media quietly backs away after offering this requisite justification: "This person has personal issues, and will be referred for counseling." So no harm done! Or the even more exquisite "the story may be false, but the problem it highlights is real." This did happen with Smollett, in fact. After the media dived headfirst into the imploding story, they were left with, "Well, Trump's racist, so—uh, so what!"

It was the thought that counts!

Fact is, if the crimes these people advocate so strongly went away, these advocates would be out of a job. It's like a trainer who prescribes you lard, in order to get you to pay for those fitness classes to burn off all that lard. (Suddenly, I'm hungry for lard.)

Of course, real hate crimes do exist. But right now it seems the demand for hate crime exceeds the supply (hell, even Amazon is sold out). How many times have we read about the noose on the doorknob, the swastika on the window, the young girl with her hair chopped off by a well-cast assailant (a

Virginia sixth grader who claimed three white male classmates held her down and cut off her dreadlocks now admits it was totally made up)—and then they all turn out to be manufactured? Numbness happens.

And the people making these hoaxes up seem on the whole to be troubled souls (what we used to call liars). And it's that fact that usually gets them off the hook. Their own inclination to commit this crime is their defense for not getting punished for that crime. Imagine if that worked for other infractions! "He robbed the bank, which reveals his sad poverty and lack of opportunity—so not guilty!"

There are two types of hoaxers:

1. Those seeking attention because they're lonely, sad, and depressed. Their act of duplicity might be a cry for help, which should get a positive response from the media. And when I see how the press reacts, I don't blame the hoaxers.

2. The conniving grifters who see the media's gullibility, and work it to help salvage their fading celebrity. Jussie Smollett's claim was hilariously improbable: a pair of white guys in MAGA hats hunting down a no-name D-list actor, in the middle of the night, in subfreezing temperatures in Chicago, carrying a noose and some

mysterious fluid. Not even the most gullible among us could believe it. But the media did! Because he was black, gay, and almost famous, the press had to pretend to believe—while everyone outside the media saw the fraud clearly. Sure, all the TV hosts suspected it was a crock, but no one in that industry wanted to be the first to say so. The risk was too much to their careers.

Smollett built a story that could have fueled a race riot. It painted a target on a group of people (Trump supporters) who had done nothing to him other than not be interested in him one iota. If he had succeeded in persuading a nation that he was telling the truth, how do you think that would have played out? If the media had had its way, we would never would have found out. The mainstream media covered Smollett's claim as if it had really happened. They hoped it had happened, in fact, since a good racial outrage might have been worth a lot of money. So what if millions of decent people who might own a red hat would have been targeted with abuse (including the Cincinnati Reds).

THE STAR PLAYER IN CANCEL CULTURE: THE SOCIAL JUSTICE WARRIOR

Social justice is a religion based on viewing the entire world through the filter of oppressor versus oppressed. And if you're not on their team, that makes you the oppressor: primed for targeting and canceling. The backbone is punishment: you've victimized me, and now you must pay.

By claiming that any opposition to their position is inherently *immoral,* they can demonize their nonviolent adversaries, personally. If branding someone with whom you disagree "evil" sounds evil, it is. Because once you remove the ability to debate ideas, then all you have left are fists, knives, and (for you citizens of Chicago and NRA members) guns. Eliminating debate removes a necessary buffer against confrontation. It might be the most regressive movement in recent history, ranking right up there with night classes in pottery.

Social justice activism attempts to silence opposing viewpoints by silencing speakers. Not the ideas. The people articulating them. For one to do this, you have to demonize.

And the media, which has hired more than a few of these warriors straight out of collegiate indoctrination camps, perpetuates this madness. Molded by graduates from the modern, toxic campus—infused by decades of social justice academic ideology—the media looks plainly at every aspect of civil society, rejects their unifying aspects, and instead points to conflict: racial, gender, political, you name it (except the fact that "short" is not a protected class—even though the tall have an edge in almost everything, apart from riding the winner at the Kentucky Derby, and hosting talk shows, apparently).

The conflict is irreparable, because no matter what one does to address the perceived injustice, it can never be enough. The goalposts are moved to the parking lot as the culprit becomes even more irredeemable. Again, this is because, once you admit your guilt, there can be no redemption. So acquiescence drives the warriors to establish even more austere standards that narrow their chosen group to an even smaller band of misery junkies. And it continues, because frankly it feels good to hurt people when you're miserable.

Back in October, I came across a study of political activists. The study, conducted by the American Enterprise Institute, found that eighteen- to thirty-five-year-olds who are lonely and socially active (yes, you can be both!) are seven times more likely than their more sociable peers to volunteer for political campaigns and groups. Also: the social young adults who aren't lonely still volunteer—but they choose faith-based groups at six times the rate as their alienated peers. In short:

people who get along with other people join organizations that the other group finds deplorable. The more lonely seek protest, the less lonely seek people (you see where this is going?).

I interviewed the guy behind the study, Ryan Streeter (you can find it on my podcast site at Fox News), and I presented to Streeter two ways to interpret his findings. The first way is a sympathetic perspective, the second a more cynical view.

My sympathetic perspective: The politically engaged person is lonely among his friends because he has larger, more pressing concerns. Sitting at the pub on trivia night with his coworkers, the thoughtful, brooding warrior can't help but think about the environment, racism, trans rights, Peru, phlebitis. His unmatched concern creates a sense of loneliness. He can't play darts or flirt with the girl who looks vaguely like Belinda Carlisle in her nineties phase, until they close down that fracking site in that other state he's never even been to. This person won't feel right around you until they solve X.

My less sympathetic perspective: Instead of antisocial behavior being a symptom of that person's need for activism, it's the reverse. Fervent activism is simply a marker for antisocial behavior. Meaning he joins a cause because no one else can stand him.

The reason that lonely people are found engaging in political activism is that they're less interested in people than they are in gaining power. As social activists, they are, oddly, distinctly antisocial. They prefer exercising demands, rather than engaging people. They're busybodies—nosy, intrusive machines of condemnation. They live for rage. Deep down they thirst for force: that they can *make* you do something, just because they can.

So in this interpretation, it's not that these people seek value in a way their pub friends don't understand, it's that they reject any sense of community. No—they prefer the lone scream. The top-volume bullhorn. They have the power of a cheerleader without the distraction of a game.

In many protests, they assume an almost robotic state as they shut down dialogue. They block things, like roads to work, trains taking kids to school, and moms rushing babies to the doctor, talk show hosts trying to pick up their prescription ointments. For a quick visual, google "Evergreen State College protests against Bret Weinstein." Then Google "Yale professor attacked over Halloween costumes." Then google "violent protesters attack professor at Middlebury College." Then google pictures of Lorenzo Lamas and send them to my work email.

In recent demonstrations over climate change, activists left boats in the middle of intersections—apparently unconcerned that their clever symbol of the apocalyptic rising tide means little to the frantic driver trying to get someone to the hospital (no worries, the patient's probably an old fat white guy whose death will only help the planet). This public intimidation unnerves people, and energizes those on the march.

I asked Streeter which one of my interpretations was wrong. I won't lie—he seemed more biased toward my cynical take, probably because it was also my more passionate one (and after all, it was my show).

It could be that radical activism is more of a marker of a type of a bitter, disturbed person, than the noble choice of an idealistic person looking out for the good of all people. In short, the concentric circles of family, religion, and community are rejected; as the SJW leapfrogs over all of them to the external gratification of public aggression and response. As Streeter points out, "Lonely young adults . . . seem much less enthused about community-based civil society." And they get rewarded for it, through their enablers, aka—you guessed it—the media.

First, the media has spent better than half a century marginalizing and ridiculing things like church, family, and community. Marriage has been deemed unnecessary, church is an oppressive influence, and small towns are a joke. The problem is that all these smart hip kids in media have offered nothing to replace these corny institutions. They have helped tear stuff down, without going the next step and replacing it with something better. Once that church is just a vacant lot, what replaces it? Will you just film your skateboard tricks there and post 'em on TikTok?

Perhaps it will take a generation to figure out that answer: What shall replace religion? Maybe it's just a better, wiser version of it. (I don't pretend to know what that is.)

THE PLUS

Go AWOL from the Stasi. Few things deliver the dopamine dose that comes with utterly destroying someone. Go to Twitter and turn the right-wing goon in by nailing him with a tweet between the eyes. Maybe a selfie with me at the beach—but with an armed stripper somewhere in the distance. The imagination that comes with righteousness will do the rest.

The problem with working the security detail for a Twitter mob is that eventually you run out of perps-of-value to your contacts in the press. You run through your list of possibles, then you start to include some friends because, who knows? They might know somebody who knows somebody who said something about Nancy or Ilhan. That is, people from whose professional demise you can profit by simply having them canceled, demolished, and exterminated.

So eventually you become an annoying left-wing sycophant, a marginal pundit spewing anger that makes no sense, because anger never does. Eventually you become Don Lemon. And from there, the bottom's the limit.

Profiting from the mistakes of others is the secret to success in Twitter—and in science.

Don't buy the hate. Treat hate crimes reported on social media with kid gloves. They're too easy to fake and the reward for faking them is too high. Take the 49 hour rule—wait 49 hours before believing anything you read. Why not 48 hours, you ask? You need an hour for lunch.

Avoid the loudest people in the room. Each side is made up of all kinds of people, and generally, within that side there's about 5 to 10 percent who are complete jerks. They're also the busiest and loudest on social media. That's because they're usually jobless and alone. But just as you don't want to be judged for the idiots on your side, don't judge your adversaries for the idiots on their side. Don't waste your time on either.

Bring people back to life. One day, I hope, that we can work backward, and "reanimate" those people that we've destroyed—dig up the bodies and zap them back to life. When you see someone trying to make a comeback after a yearlong humiliation, meet them with an outstretched hand, not a mocking tweet.

Don't write for free. Unless you're in the media or entertainment—no one pays you to publicly express your thoughts. Yet each post risks the paycheck you have. You can have a pretty good job at an accounting firm, but one unacceptable media opinion gone viral, and you're back temping at your uncle's lawn care company. And you're terrible at lawn care.

And no, it doesn't matter how noble your job might be. Firemen, paramedics, nurses, police officers, priests—they've all lost jobs because of a single slip on social media. (The slips could warrant a firing, of course: who wants to have someone in the office advocating Machete Night? The only people safe from this, of course, are liberal commentators, primarily named Joy. See Joy Behar, and Joy Reid. The two Joys seem immune. I should change my name to Joy Gutfeld.)

Get off it without getting off on it. I tell myself I will quit social media but that's like saying, "I'm going to leave health insurance." I hate the mess of it all, but I'm stuck with it. So instead, I treat it like one would treat *ideal* health insurance: focus on only what you need. Follow the people who are a plus to your life. Meaning those who don't upset you, but instead make you better and happy. By the way, I don't mean people who tweet inspirational quotes or gauzy shots of sunsets. They're actually worse than Russian troll farms. I'm talking about cultivating a farm of smart, giving people you can bleed dry. Which means . . .

Be a leech. Leeching is what social media is for. Leeching is what we are all for. If you see every person around you as a plus, then you can subtract what you need to make your day easier. It's like lowering your carb count by increasing protein. Conversely, avoid minuses—people who spend so much time on negative stuff, conspiracies, desperate causes, or alarming stores and scares. Generally, we all have one crazy aunt in our lives; you don't need to create an army of them.

Read the news; don't make any. Other than buying this book, you get nothing for showing off your intellectual prowess or your sparkling good humor. Here's why: according to one seasoned humorist (he shall remain anonymous and therefore leech-worthy), approximately one-third of the population can't tell the difference between a joke and a serious statement. We can call it the Adam Schiff rule. See, what appears to be funny in your brainpan turns out to be the opposite in his.

My life is a nonstop series of people taking me seriously, when really, I was only kidding (I actually didn't invent penicillin, although I was a famous Mexican toreador and have the pants to prove it). I joke a lot, but in this world, there are approximately 2.5 billion people who won't get it.

Take this advice to the bank. My best advice for all social media commentary? Safety deposit it. Nothing good ages well, unless your name is Talisker. So if you've got an awesome joke, then if it's so awesome, email it to yourself, and wait at least three hours. Chances are, you'll return to it, and find it stale and somewhat smelly (which is what happens to anything you leave alone for three hours). However, if you're thinking, "Wow, this is even better than I remember!" then the stuff is pure gold, or you hit your head.

Press record. Better to be safe if you're ever accused. We live in an era where what we hated may end up saving us: surveillance. How ironic is it that the thing a libertarian might find intrusive could be the only thing that protects libertarians from the do-gooders around us? (Answer: very ironic.) I'm not even sure what I'm suggesting, but if you're accused by some freak of doing something that you didn't do, closed-circuit security cameras may be the only thing that can clear your name. How many stories have you seen where an accusation is disproved by released footage? Imagine how many falsely accused people had their lives ruined because there was no tape? We need tape. Lots of it. Surveillance doesn't limit us; it frees us from the clutches of liars.

FOUR PLUSES TO TATTOO ON YOUR FOREHEAD

When someone screws up, define them by their best intentions, not their worst. Because for the most part, people are trying to do their best.

If something ugly from a person's past reveals itself, wait before you crucify. If someone is genuinely remorseful, and the infraction was long ago, let it slide. Even if they won't return the favor.

Defend people who don't like you. It means more than simply defending your buddies.

Share the risk. If a friend is in trouble and attracting a mob of haters, offer support on your friend's behalf. The more who do this, the higher the price it is for the mob to commit to their mob action. Do not follow this advice of course, if your friend did something truly heinous (like leaving a bad review of my book on Amazon).

The great thing about risk sharing is it's contagious. It's like herd immunity! When someone under attack finds support from others, then it becomes easier for others to join in and do the same. Your crowd of sympathetic supporters will grow exponentially as one person after another says, "Oh, right. Now I remember." The angry mob finds strength and anonymity in numbers, but the fact is, their numbers are limited. Besides, their mob is composed of bullies by definition. And what do we know about bullies? Right. They fold when threatened. Most people don't want to ban a college speaker or a conservative pundit. But they don't want to speak up against the smaller tide, either. But by sharing the risk, and defending others from attack, you create a growing army of decent people. And the more people who share the risk, the smaller their shares become. Supporting people like Dave Rubin, whose cancellation from the left turned him into a podcast innovator, shows you what can happen when we share the risk, instead of running from it. And he was able to do that because a number of people came forward to defend him. It's a great message for those who fear cancellation: you can find a second, newer, and more enriching life once you've been expunged. Comedians like Andrew Schulz, Dave Chappelle, and Bill Burr are their own bosses—in effect making it impossible for the outrage gluttons to get them fired. Burr can't fire himself; instead he can make bank pointing out that very fact to his delighted fans.

THE PLUS: THE TALK OF THE STREET

Activists often come with baggage that drives their inner turmoil. That turmoil speaks. Sometimes it even stinks. But if you keep your distance, you'll find it's easier to avoid hearing the nonsense. So the best you can do is to keep stepping back, until you're on the other side of the street, where they can't spit on you. A friend of mine told me his no-fail way to deal with street annoyers. One day in front of the United Nations headquarters on Second Avenue, he found himself surrounded by a dozen or so bad-tempered demonstrators. They kept shouting at him as he retreated. Finally, he turned on them and shouted, "Dumb fuck, I don't speak English!" They stopped, shrugged, and left.

Help, My (Sister, Son, Uncle) Is an SJW!

If you see a family member or friend veering into extreme politics, it's up to you to offer more attractive alternatives. It's probably too idealistic to think a boxing class would have kept Junior from joining antifa—but we must realize that antifa really is a boxing class for people who've never hit anyone except with a stick. Street aggression offers the same rush as sports, so maybe it's worth a shot, before writing someone off, to get them another physical outlet. If boxing is too rough, maybe they can try Ping-Pong. It's like boxing, but without the hitting. Yeah, okay, its not like boxing.

Personally, I always go back to music. It's such a simple plus that replaces so many minuses. I've seen it change lives, one annoying folksinger at a time. If hip-hop can turn drug-dealing gangbangers into raging capitalists, then everything is possible. I myself was an angry young man until I took up the didgeridoo.

CHAPTER 6

DESTROY THE DESIRE TO IMITATE

Back in September 2019, a plane crashed in Turkey, Texas (yes, there is such place). The two passengers suffered only minor injuries. Hooray for that. Not so hooray-ish: the reason for the crash. It was caused by a gender reveal stunt gone awry. (For those unaware, a "gender reveal" party is a public announcement by expectant parents of the sex of their unborn child— kind of insurance against abortion. You have to go farther north and east for "abortion reveal" parties.) Apparently the pilot was flying at a low altitude, in order to release 350 gallons of pink water for the reveal, which caused the plane to slow and stall. The plane ended up slamming into the ground. Thankfully no one died, and 350 gallons of free water in Texas can be a bonus.

We can't say the same thing for the fifty-six-year-old woman who, a few weeks later, was killed by a flying piece of debris, caused by an explosion that was part of another gender reveal party.

I've been circling a topic for some time: mimetic theory. Like everything that sounds super important, the phrase comes from a Greek word—in this case "mimesis." According to my buddy Google, mimesis (pronounced "mim-EE-sis") means "imitation and representation," which says that "people are influenced by each other and the world around them."

Mind-blowing, right? I'm not sure we needed Socrates for that, but whatever.

Well, it kinda is. Because once you see how much behavior is copied—you can no longer mentally escape it. It's everywhere. And we're not talking good behavior, but mediocre behavior, and even awful crap, like crashing planes in order to announce the gender of someone's potential brat. We copy each other, and we can't stop.

On *The Five*, I ban phrases that reach the threshold of annoying repetition. I didn't realize it at the time, but I've always been grossed out by mimesis—and my distaste for it has gotten me fired three times from great occupations (I'm sure the Greeks had a word for that, too). Because I didn't want to do what other magazines, or editors, or publishers did—and because I thought that the usual public relations kowtowing was garbage—I would inevitably get the heave-ho. So, now, on *The Five* I direct that energy into banning phrases like "let's unpack this topic," "you can't make this up," or "at the end of the day." But there's something unfair about my hatred. Everyone has an innate nature to belong, which fuels the desire to replicate behaviors that seem advantageous. But my real hatred isn't for you, it's for the mimetic media whose desire to belong ends up fueling bad ideas and stupid causes. Look at the media who fell all over themselves, slipping on their own drool, chasing the creepy litigious lollipop known as Michael Avenatti. Every anchor (except the FNC ones) saw him as their answer to Trump—which created a moral blindness that would have been comical if it weren't so grotesque. So where is this media's next great hope, as I write this very word? In the same prison cell once occupied by El Chapo. And where are all of his media lackeys, who like mimetic lemmings rushed to get selfies with him, while bathing him in gooey praise?

They're nowhere to be found. True media friends! He went from lover to leper in seconds.

It's clear that the natural human desire is to belong: a survival mechanism to get our genes into its next iteration leads us to imitate each other. Fitting in keeps you from being killed. People who deviate from acceptable behavior are ostracized—

thrown to the wolves, tossed over the wall, chased to the woods, forced to create Goth bands and do inventory in the basement of the local Hot Topic (I got fired from that, too). The "imitating of the horde" makes those who don't (for either mental or moral reasons) seem especially weird.

High school (and now college) is one big mimetic magnet, where we learn to do three things:

- imitate the leader

- imitate those who imitate the leader

- hide from those who see you aren't imitating the leader

Once, imitation meant survival. Which is why, right around fifth grade, I lost all my friends. (I wrote about this in an earlier book, *Not Cool.*) When I refused to join a gang in which all members would behave like sharks, I was ostracized for a year, maybe longer. I know you're wondering what this has to do with "gender reveal." Well, how does something as idiotic as dumping gallons of pink water while putting assorted lives in danger actually happen? It happens mimetically. And it grows mimetically. One person sees the favorable attention received for one reveal. He likes the idea, then decides to replicate it—only making it better, bigger, more memorable. And any stunt involving an airplane is by definition a bad idea. We should all know this by now.

So you begin by popping a balloon filled with pink or blue glitter (which itself is problematic these days: how dare you assign such oppressive colors, which is nothing more than a social construct born of the patriarchy!), then progressing to slicing a cake to find pink or blue filling. And, voilà, thanks to mimetic competition, you end up with a plane flipping over in a field. Thank God it missed heavy traffic. This stupid "event" risked ending the lives of many whose gender was already fairly established—that is, the people walking around below it. All of them likely couldn't care less about the baby in question. I mean, talk about self-important. This will be the most self-important child since that Swedish kid who's always going on about climate change. (Shouldn't she be off yodeling or something?)

I suppose I could have used the "Tide Pod challenge" as an example of mimetic idiocy, but that has one extra variable: smaller, adolescent brains. And I'm not entirely sure it took off as a trend, except among the attention-addict YouTubers. It may have been more media hysteria than anything.

Sadly, though, there are adults doing this stuff—which shows you the sheer power of mimetic desire, and the weakness of modern adults. Our culture creates psychological Benjamin Buttons, adults reversing in maturity as they try to imitate teenagers more and more.

This desire holds more control over us than sex and food. Because imitation is the key to getting both. In order to get sex and food, we gotta be accepted. Why do you think God made letterman's jackets?

I've written about low-slung jeans before, but it remains a unique example of how mimetic behavior's charm transcends utility. I mean, it's hard to run with a waistband at your thighs, and it's hard to carry anything when your left or right hand must continually tug at the belt loop of your sagging pants (it's why I had to leave the Crips). This behavior won't get you a job, except maybe making license plates. And everyone will blame "societal factors" instead of that invisible internal drive to belong.

Facial tattoos might have initially meant some sort of daring rebellion—but not now that every mediocre white hip-hopper is doing it. I mean, when some kid named Corey is getting a teardrop below his eyelid, and a spiderweb tattoo on his neck, maybe that *is* progress. There was a point in time when a teardrop tattoo meant, "I killed someone in prison." Now it means, "I get to my tech job on a Razor scooter." (I came across a great headline this November morning in the

New York Post: "Sarah Hyland shares painful experience of having butt tattoo removed." In that headline alone you are left with one question: Who is Sarah Hyland?)

Tattoos used to be the bastion of warriors, soldiers, and bikers, but now they're the product of a drunken actress intent on spicing up her Instagram. Problem: barbed wire biceps mean so little when the guy down the block has Satan on his face. Mimetic desire kills all rebellious action by simply spreading the behavior so it's no longer rebellious, which only encourages more intense attempts at outdoing each other (you got a face tattoo? Ha—I just pierced my uvula!).

This is something super important to note when you're on social media, or on campus—or hell, anywhere—in which a mob is taking hold of the conversation. Mimetic action is contagious, but you never really saw it before. Now you do. And that's good. For it tells you not to engage. To combat the excesses of mimesis, the action is simple: *Do not join.* And if possible, offer support to those who are being harpooned by the joiners.

When you see one person surrounded by many, remember that your action makes it easier for others to follow. And harder for others not to. You have the power to reverse mimetic gravity. You can turn it on itself. Which is really what this book is all about.

To fight mimesis, it's pretty simple.

Ask yourself, are you copying someone else's behavior? Be honest with yourself. You may not even know you're doing it until you ask yourself that question (asking yourself this question because I asked you to is not mimesis!).

If three or more people are doing X, and you're compelled to join—step back and consider why. If X is expressing an opinion, it's only because the barrier to entry is low in agreeing with that opinion, which may not even be a real opinion, or one held strongly. Maybe it's just a "thing" that is an opinion in a gaseous state. Walk on by: nothing to see here.

But if what a group is doing appears to be a good thing (like lifting a car off a trapped pedestrian), I wouldn't worry too much about the flaws of mimetic desire! Copying good behavior ain't a bad thing, in general. (We are doing it now in this countrywide lockdown.) Unless it's perceived as good by the media—then it's just vacuous virtue-signaling in order to appear superior and grab some easy attention.

How do we fight mimesis, when it's really all over the place? Well, think about how it informs our behavior growing up. How much of it is constructed to keep us from being ourselves, and from taking risks that might make us better people. Now it's bigger because it has a friend in social media echo chambers, and it's why adults are now not growing out of the behavior.

But let's go back to where it really begins. In that hellhole called the classroom.

EDUCATING DOWN

In November 2019, Kamala Harris made a bold promise—that if she were elected, she would try to lengthen the school day for kids, in order to match the schedules of their working parents. When I heard it initially, I offered an agreeable nod. I mean, keeping kids in class until 6 p.m.? That means fewer punks on the street between three and six—and there's nothing more frightening than marauding brats roaming the road, looking to unload their uncaged energy on world-class celebrities like myself. (The worst part about teens in a group? You punch one in the face, and suddenly you're the bad guy! I maintain that when one teen becomes two teens, this negates any age difference, and you can hit them if they come at you. Just make sure you're not just *seeing* two teens.) If I had my way, school would be twenty-four hours, seven days a week, held in a meat locker one hundred leagues under the sea.

But then I had an epiphany—sparked by a brilliant random tweet by a chap named Frank J. Fleming, in response to Harris's idea. He tweeted: "If your only job was to learn for the next 16 years, you'd expect to come out of that like Batman. For kids, we're happy if after K-12 plus college, they have one marketable skill. Most of the school time is already just wasted busywork, but they want to increase it?"

So, there was more wisdom in that small pile of words than shelves of books on education and homeschooling. I imagine myself at eight years old, and some mysterious man (me, from the future) walks into my room and asks, "What three things really interest you? For the next sixteen years, you will devote six hours a day to that."

Well, I loved TV talk shows (Merv Griffin, Dinah Shore, Mike Douglas, *Fernwood 2 Night*) and I loved horror movies (anything with Vincent Price). I worshipped punk rock (it was the mid to late 1970s, after all) and crank calls (I wrote my own). I also loved boxing, and had a pair of gloves when I was eight. Finally I also had the strange habit of setting my alarm for 5 a.m. so I could lie in bed until seven and think about the world. (I did that every day for years. Now I get paid to do it.)

Now, we know how much sixteen years really is. You can do more than learn one thing—you can be a master at a few things—if you choose wisely and according to your desires. Think about a six-hour day of "classes" that begins at eight years old and is designed to teach you just three things:

- 2 hours in the morning on martial arts

- 2 hours in the afternoon on electric guitar and/or public speaking

- 2 hours on philosophy and religion

Sixteen years later, at twenty-four, what would you, or I, have been—barring any tragic accident, debilitating disease, or drug addiction? And also, without the filler of standard education to eat up your days, and years?

Well, sixteen years of that curriculum would yield a Bruce Lee/Jimi Hendrix/Yoda hybrid. You or me could kill a man three times our size, play "Purple Haze" on a Strat behind our necks, while positing the differences between the world's major Sophists.

In a very real sense, as Fleming says in his much simpler tweet, you and I would be Batman. We, in fact, would be a nation of Batmans, and Batwomans—Bat-folk.

Instead, the average twenty-five-year-old panics over whether he has the aptitude for a job interview in pharmaceutical sales.

THE PLUS

Don't make goals. I remember the mistakes I made in life—and they're a combination of goal-making and time-wasting. At eighteen, I told myself that in a decade, at twenty-eight, I would be X (a renowned writer). Ten years seemed like enough time to reach that goal (which it is), which also made it an easy amount of time to goof off. The more time you have, the more time you waste (look at any drum solo). And it may not be a bad thing. I read about research on procrastination that said it's life telling you that whatever you're putting off, you really don't have to do. If the bullet's coming at you, you probably won't hesitate to think about ducking.

Fact is, death is the bullet and it's on the way. So move it.

Like most people, you probably don't reach a goal unless you start doing stuff bit by bit—staring at a goal from far away offers you little beyond an intimidating sense of possible failure.

Scott Adams has made this point first: outsize goals suck because you're bound to fail. Start with easy success. You don't need to rule the world before lunch. You just need to make your bed, as Jordan Peterson keeps reminding us.

I wanted to star in a TV show when I was in second grade.

I did a puppet show based on the Watergate hearings and no one laughed at either version. I wrote a game show play for an eighth-grade talent show that offended the audience of moms and dads, but also surprised my parents (it was called "Up Your Income," and I wore my mother's wig when I played the host; at the end of the show, the contestants either beat me up or kill me—it's a matter of interpretation; oddly, now that I think about it—I haven't traveled far from that). I think that was the first time I revealed to the outside world what was inside my mind. I was a smart, moody kid (girls would call me "weird")—I could ace a spelling bee in my sleep, especially if the words was "zzzz"—but this was the first time I walked in front of a group of people and took a real risk in revealing who I was. I was coming out as a madman, in my mom's wig.

I wish that someone had come along and said to me at that age, "Hey kid—you're twelve. You wanna do *that* for a living? Sixteen years from now, we're gonna do that every day for two hours. If you lose the wig." I would have cried with happiness. Instead, I took courses in geometry. And I lost the wig, too.

If my dreams had matched my education, who knows how things might have turned out? If I'd played my cards just a little differently, I could have had a talk show at thirty, a drug addiction at thirty-five, and been dead at thirty-eight. Instead, I started my TV career full-on at forty-two. And that was thirteen years ago. If he'd known what was coming, that little Greg sitting in his room in the 1970s watching *Fernwood 2 Night* would be over the moon.

Be bad. The secret to becoming great at anything isn't just wanting to be great, but a willingness to be bad, and to keep being bad for a long time. It took me years to figure that out. In fact, I took a roundabout path of being good (editing magazines) before I risked being bad (hosting TV shows). Weird thing: it was my job in publishing that threw me under the TV bus. At a certain point, publishers had enough of my reverse mimetic obnoxiousness. I started doing guest hits on Headline News, MTV, and VH1 ("Paris Hilton—what's up with her?" was my go-to line; and yes, I'm aware it doesn't resonate like it used to), and it became clear that even though magazines were not prepping me for the camera, my ability to run meetings did—especially when I decided to hire "little people" to liven things up a little. Everything I did at the annual meeting of the American Society of Magazine Editors (google it) on *Red Eye* or *The Five* and on *The Greg Gutfeld Show* was about passing the ball, teasing each other, and giving people something to talk about.

So, now I'm fifty-five. Christ, I can't believe I'm not in jail or dead. But you have to believe in something. But in another sixteen years, I'll be seventy-one and looking forward to a stent.

So now I've started playing guitar again, and by the time I'm seventy-one, if I'm not an Ensure-drinking, Stairlift-using Eric Clapton, I'll eat my Life Alert.

That's the answer . . .

START YOUR OWN CURRICULUM

Our education system has sold us one way of learning, and it's a waste of precious life. The only way to combat American education is to start your own education department. We're doing it now—at least I'm doing it now. The Internet is the world's biggest, free college—and no one has figured that out yet. (This includes, of all places, YouTube. The moment they start a deal with accreditations, it's completely over for Harvard, which couldn't happen to a nicer bunch of bullshit artists.)

How do you think I'm learning the Cramps catalog on guitar? Do you think I actually have a teacher? No, I have YouTube. I'm learning philosophy; the ins and outs of artificial intelligence and how to play the "Free Bird" solo (which is way easier than it sounds but not easy to do simultaneously). I still can't play speed metal (neither can most speed metalists—that's the point) but in a month, I'll be doing the entire Anthrax catalog—and I'll know how to properly frame the selfie I'll take while bungee-jumping off a 747.

The experts are now there for the clicking, and anyone can learn from one, to become one.

So the answer is to create your own curriculum. It's easy as one, two, three:

1. Tonight: pick three things you're interested in learning more about. They cannot include DIY neurosurgery or an old girlfriend who should have never broken up with you. But otherwise, that's all.

2. Then tomorrow, enter "introduction to (subject one)" to YouTube. That's your first class.

3. Then, each night do it again. Three classes, a different one every night.

Maybe Monday is stoicism. Tuesday is beginner guitar. Wednesday is public speaking.

Set your own pace, so that at your leisure, by 2050, you'll be a fearless stoic who can explain why you are going to play "Layla" in front of thousands. You'll be Batman. And you never saw it coming.

WHAT HAPPENS WHEN YOU TURN SCHOOL FROM A MINUS TO A PLUS?

I no longer watch the Grammys, because like my receding hairline it reminds me how old I am. I know none of the nominees—except the young woman who basically and historically swept all the major categories. Billie Eilish and her older brother Finneas O'Connell cleaned up at the Grammys.

In an interview with "Your Teen Media" (my go-to for all things teen media), O'Connell had this to say about (gulp) homeschooling: "Being homeschooled is all about self-discovery. It's something that I've really enjoyed and thrived under. I'm not at a high school where I have to base my self-worth off what other people think of me. . . . I think that's an enormously positive thing."

What is he talking about? He's talking about escaping the pressure of mimetic desire, which forces everyone to belong, and do the same thing, even if you're better at something else. He rejected that. And he was able to carve out a unique education for himself that made him and his sister stars.

"Everybody's always out doing things, traveling, going places, meeting for classes, and organizing field trips. . . .

You take what you want, where you want it, and you find what you need . . ."

With that kind of control over life's curriculum, maybe it's not such a surprise he and sister hit upon such monstrous success so early in their lives. Think about it. They were allowed to chase their dreams, not chained to crappy little desks and told what to believe and what to memorize.

Maybe that's where the answer lies. Who needs school?

According to *Reason* magazine, about 3.3 percent of K–12 students are homeschooled, or about 1.7 million. The most common reason for homeschooling is worries over safety, drugs, or peer pressure. As writer Michael Malice often says, and I paraphrase, school is probably the only place you will ever encounter violence in your life. Does that ring true for you? It did for me. (I once arm-wrestled the school nurse for painkillers.)

CHAPTER 7

WHAT DOESN'T OFFEND YOU MAKES YOU STRONGER

If you're an honest person, if you're an abrasive person, or even if you're—dare I say it—an obnoxious and sometimes offensive person—okay, if you're a *real* person—then you are living in dangerous times. Or borrowed time, too.

Never before—at least in my half century on this planet— have I experienced a time when silly things you say can end your career, or even worse, shame you into oblivion. We live in a time where anyone at any time can ask you a question, and if you answer it with an honest opinion, you can be held liable for crimes of simply answering a question with an honest opinion, unless your opinion resembles the crazy, over-the-top opinions of, say, Paul Krugman, in which case, you'll become the genius guest on a million podcasts that nobody will listen to.

But if you tell a joke, it could end up being your last laugh. A joke is only funny to those who are not angry. And a joke can be deadly serious if those who hear it want it to be. Simply take it out of context and the joke becomes your epitaph. Humor has become the West's purity test.

Today is a time of the humorless tyranny: in which a small band of rage merchants are exterminating all possibilities for the one thing that holds us together: jokes, conversation, teasing. In the (once again, mythical) good old days (of, say, ten years ago) one could break the tension with a wisecrack. Two men at a bar can alleviate conflict over who gets served first by joking about it. A commuter can reduce the potential for violence on a train by diverting to self-deprecation. Humor served as some sort of evolutionary survival mechanism: if you had the joke gene in you, you were shielded from the rocks thrown by the other tribe. Funny was a skill along with strength and speed. You were vital to keeping the peace and entertaining cave-dwellers, and later, kings and commanders. There's a reason court jester became a career path in the time when "a good day" meant you hadn't been sodomized by Visigoths.

Today, it seems we want to remove the obstacle between emotion and violence. We want to remove the tool that makes things run smoothly, that brings people together, that reduces differences into things we can laugh about. Jewish comedians, for example, were able to bring their culture to a more mainstream audience by laughing about parts of it with that wider audience.

So we are subtracting the thing that unites us, and adding the toxin of grievance.

How did this start?

I have a theory.

This one-way demonization has been around for decades. My guess is it really took off after the Vietnam War. Where such violent actions propagated by America weren't perceived as simply wrong-headed, but *evil*. You weren't just someone who wanted to fight communism—you were also a baby killer. I don't believe this kind of thinking really existed regarding the Korean War, or the two big wars before it. Or the Civil or Revolutionary wars. Or the War of the Roses, for that matter. But if you went to Vietnam, something was clearly wrong *with you*. Guys came back from battle and were vilified by those jerks they had been ordered to defend.

The Left championed this approach, even though Democrats started that war! And a Republican ended it. Unconstrained progressives, drunk on the power of rectitude, took this idea and ran with it through the 1970s, '80s, '90s, and right up to today! *If the other side is evil, how on earth can you laugh about it?*

You may think that the demonization of Trump is unique, but only if you weren't around to see how the media portrayed Barry Goldwater, Ronald Reagan, Bushes 1 and 2, and anyone to the right of Jane Fonda. Even the blandest guy on earth, Mitt Romney, was portrayed as a bully, misogynist, and an animal abuser. Remember the dog in the carrier on the roof? Back then, the media believed that story legitimately disqualified Romney from running for president. (Then again, it *is* kinda weird.)

So now we are here, and all around us, we see people being singled out online and in real life for infractions we used to dismiss as honest mistakes, or perhaps jokes. They are forced to apologize, and even then, that is not enough when they do. They are banished for their sins.

This is no unserious trend. It's actually a symptom of a disease, and part of an orchestrated action to undo what holds us together.

Civilization. Without humor, there is no such thing as civilization. It levels all disputes to human scale. Just look at what that clown Aristophanes, the Mel Brooks of old Athens, did to august Socrates. It's what Ricky Gervais did to Hollywood at the Golden Globes. If you believe that the other side is wrong, you can laugh it off. But if you think it's not just wrong but *evil*, then sooner or later, laughter must be banned. Because humor, by uniting different perspectives, results in "normalizing" people you don't like. People you see as evil.

"Normalizing." It's the word of the media mob, and it means essentially "making something evil less evil by talking to it."

Would you like me to use it in sentence? Sure thing:

"By inviting Donald Trump onto his show and tussling his hair, Jimmy Fallon normalized the evil that is that profane, offensive man."

I wrote that off the top of my head but I read variations of it at least a dozen times. I plugged "normalizing Trump" into the Google machine and found thousands of results. Including these headlines you could have designed yourself:

"Despite all the warnings, we are normalising Donald Trump"

(It's from a left-wing British paper, *The Guardian*, hence the spelling.)

"It's too late to worry about 'normalizing' Trump."

From *Rolling Stone*, a periodical so apocalyptic, it's beyond hope to even worry!

"The insidious psychology of normalizing Donald Trump."

This, from *The New Republic*, gets bonus points for using "insidious psychology."

And there's this one:

"President Trump is normalizing racism." This one is a twofer—the normalization and the bigot card, tied together. I'm sure the *Washington Post* writer got a pay raise for that.

Meanwhile, Trump supporters were having fun. Telling jokes. Enjoying rallies. Teasing their friends. The Dean Wormer effect had finally been reversed. Meaning: now it was the Left who became the sourpuss character from *Animal House*, and the rest of us became the fun-loving Bluto. The residents of Animal House are Always Trumpers. Dean Wormer is a Never Trumper.

In sum, you can't be funny, if you're evil. And if you're evil, you can't be funny. (I suddenly sound like one of these Greeks I've been referencing.)

This doesn't bode well for us as a people. Because a path to conflict is the product of a refusal to compromise. Once you categorize people as good or evil, you create a battle that pits person against person. An opposing view is no longer simply disagreeable; it's a cause for war, it's cause for death.

And targeting humor is a sign that this is coming. And it's a real threat to civilization. But the problem in explaining this threat is in the gathering of the examples one needs to make the point. There are just too damn many. So just as I'm getting going, I have to start all over again because a new outrage hops along. Trying to keep tabs on all the examples of joke-policing and joke-punishment is like trying to count screams on a roller coaster.

We are now punishing jokes—both good and bad—into extinction.

I was going to begin with the leaked morbid joke about Senator McCain (it was reported that allegedly Trump had joked that John McCain's opposition to CIA nominee Gina Haspel really didn't matter because he was dying soon).

This outrage, much like the Donald Trump "shithole" line or the "grab them by the pussy" line, was an overheard statement, not meant for public consumption. You could find all of these lines offensive or wrong, but for me, the idea of finking on people bugs me more. We all say awful things in private—we even make jokes about the dead and the dying. We do this precisely because *they are too awful*. To make a horrible joke about someone's death—see, the joke *is* that *it is a horrible joke about someone's death.* The more over-the-top something is, the more we actually don't mean it. It used to be that the first (and usually the best) jokes about a disaster came from the class clowns on Wall Street. The worse the disaster, the funnier the joke.

Remember Gilbert Gottfried's infamous Twitter cascade following the Japanese earthquake? He sent out a slate of sick jokes (example: "I just split up with my girlfriend, but like the Japanese say, 'they'll be another one floating by any minute now'").

Do you think he was truly wishing ill will on anyone? No, he was playing with the idea of "too soon," and pushing it to such an absurd degree that it was fundamentally meaningless. But, it turns out it was "too soon," and his career was nearly ruined. These days, even the joke, "too soon," is too soon. And I really like Gilbert Gottfried. I'm taller than him and we have the same initials.

I feel bad watching comedians getting ruined for doing their job, which is to take risks and sometimes cross lines. I feel worse when no one goes to bat for them.

THE PLUS

Take a joke. Finally, in 2019, we saw a glimpse of a solution to this weirdness—when *Saturday Night Live*'s Pete Davidson flippantly mocked Congressman Dan Crenshaw's war wound on Weekend Update, saying it was received "in a war or whatever."

Davidson caught holy hell for a joke that was meant on its

face to be deliberately awful. Davidson, no stranger to loss (his firefighter dad died on 9/11), knew that the casual dismissal of the Navy SEAL's permanent injury (the eye patch tells you the obvious) was meant to be funny by its awfulness. Therefore, if Davidson didn't actually know he was saying something awful, then it wouldn't be funny. But this point is too subtle: and Davidson incurred wrath from all sides, including me. The situation was remedied smartly when rising star Crenshaw showed up the following week to chat with troubled star Davidson, live on *SNL*. This is *progress*. We need more of this stuff.

But it's also a tell. Consider: Would anyone on the left who had been "offended" by a joke ever show up to undercut that joke's effect? You think if I made a sexist joke about, say, Kamala Harris, would she do anything other than demand I be crucified and cite me as "yet another example of 'Trump normalizing sexism'?" The disdain the Left has for the unwashed evil conservatives leaves them no room to laugh with us. Least of all at themselves.

What's most important is that Crenshaw didn't demand an apology; nobody needed to hear the concerned take from anyone, after that. Crenshaw actually dismissed the reflexive nature to scream outrage at every affront, even if it comes from his side (the right, which a lot of it did).

There were a lot of lessons from this incident that the rest of society needs to learn. Sadly there's a group of rage-aholics who refuse to hear. But here goes:

1. Realize the awfulness of something *is* the actual joke.

2. Realize no one is actually trying to hurt anyone.

3. Realize you look way cooler when you don't ask for an apology.

4. And if the joke has nothing to do with you, demanding an apology makes you look like an attention-seeking oaf pretending to be a white knight.

I like to remind people that jokes are just jokes—even when they aren't funny. Especially when they aren't funny. Because jokes usually only strike you as "not funny" when they strike too close to home. If you believe a joke offends you—laugh. *What doesn't offend you makes you stronger.*

It's more about our responses to jokes than the jokes themselves. For we seem to be creating, even celebrating, our purges and our not-so-secret policing, and the results could be long-lasting and highly destructive. And certainly, a lot less funny.

CHAPTER 8

CONCLUSION

How to Finally End Polarization
(the chapter where I pretend to end polarization!)

I've hammered the nail of polarization until my right thumb is powder, but one thing I failed to mention: it's a lie that we don't enjoy polarization. Some minuses just can't become pluses. Come on—if we all hated polarization so much, it wouldn't exist at all. We wouldn't have tennis or Ping-Pong. Can we agree on that? The fact is, polarization is super fun. We love antagonism as a spectator sport, and we even like participating in it. Almost every single reality talent show has that as its principal engine. Whether it's talent judges, or the contestants themselves, we gravitate toward the commotion of an angry, flashy personality (or a cantankerous smirking ape like me).

I compare it to a sport, because for a lot of people it *is* a sport. It's a game, one you can play for fun, or for money. I do it for a living, as you know. I had no idea I would end up playing pro-polarization, but I'm not going lie: I think I impart good times and some wisdom while I do it. It beats mowing lawns or tarring roofs—two things I was very bad at. But I can argue like nobody's business. And really, it's none of your business.

However, unlike other professional sports, polarization can be played year-round, 24/7, with only breaks for the bed, the bath, and beyond. And that's been the issue with this recent, most harrowing era of polarization. It's essentially nonstop—tripling the volume of back-and-forth. How did this happen? I've alluded to it before, but it's a combination of factors:

Donald Trump.

Donald Trump.

Donald Trump.

Not really.

But really.

NO, yes.

No! YES!

Screw you!

See, he even makes me argue with myself over his impact of polarization! But here's how it really came about. In the pre-Trump era, public political warfare was essentially a one-way street. Sure, Republicans and Democrats tangled in debates and smeared each other in ads—but in terms of bare-knuckled brawling, the Democrats ran that alley like seasoned tattooed sailors covered in cinnamon and oregano (a little daydream I sometimes indulge in). But today, Trump's aggressiveness and inability to find any high road (why should he when they don't, either, he'll ask—and he's got a point) means all the fights you were never really aware of happening are now taking place right in front of you. Yep, Mom and Dad are now quarreling loudly in public, right in the housewares aisles of Costco. And we're learning so much about everything that we never knew before! I mean, these public fights Trump has engaged in always leave me with something I didn't really go deep on before—whether it's stuff about China, or NAFTA, or the donor class, or the nepotistic benefits of political power. But the crap sure gets loud, and it's exhausting and it never ends.

To that complaint, I say to my liberal friends, now you know how we felt when we went to college, or watched the Oscars, or turned on network news. You did this to us on a regular basis, so give us a break here.

We've always felt like the odd person out, the one getting harangued. But now that one-way street has gone two-way. And it may not have improved relationships (that would take a three-way), but it corrected for something, like improving the flow of ideas. I do realize that the correction might be an overcorrection—but I'm struggling now to see how to fix that.

First, try to see how different the past would be if you simply replaced any American political leader with Trump. The Left branded George W. Bush a war criminal, based on the Iraq incursion. How would Trump have dealt with that, if he were the target? Would he ignore it? Probably not. My guess is (and this is hard to do because I'm imagining Trump defending a war he was against, so my eyes are twitching a bit) he would call his critics "sick," and "in bed with terrorists," and "people who don't care if radical extremist Islamists come to your city and bomb the crap out your schools" IDIOTS!

That's what I think he would have said, and that war criminal label would have been muted.

But maybe you don't remember that the smear "war criminal" is used on just about all Republicans once they reach power. For their adversaries, it's the logical extension of "hawk," the same way people like me used to make the logical extension of "liberal" into "commie scum." (Note: many still do exercise this habit, but I try to cut mine down to only three times a week—I'm really evolving!) But Reagan was painted as Hitler; John McCain was a neocon warmonger; Mitt Romney got off easier because he was no threat, so they painted him a scissor-wielding bully who abused a dog. All of these smears worked to an extent (not so much on Reagan—there was no Twitter yet—and besides, he loved horses), but I doubt they would have made much of a dent on Trump. Because he punches back when he sees your punch coming. And really, he can't help himself, can he? It's why he got elected, so it's part of that package—and complaining about it, still . . . seems like re-litigating an old divorce. Instead of scratching at old wounds, why not learn from the damn experience? There's a lot there.

But consider that even in times of war—when planes were coming back with coffins draped in flags—the polarization never reached this pitch. Was it because either the Republicans were bad at fighting back, or couldn't be bothered? Who knows (we do), but now it's different. It's loud, crazy, and mean, and very, very public. So, how do you proceed? What if it bothers you? Or your spouse? Or your friends who love you, but hate Trump. Or what if you hate Trump and your friends don't?

I'm going to say this while knocking on wood (so I'm typing this with one hand right now): the first sentence of the earlier paragraph mentioned a stark fact: we had thousands of war dead, and calmer discourse. Now we have (again, knock on wood) no thousands of war dead, and insane discourse.

Wouldn't you call that a pretty fair trade? A trade that you would take in a millisecond?

What does that tell you? Maybe that the discourse is just that; the rhetoric that floods our airwaves and streets is not directly related to outcomes that cause physical suffering and grief. I do understand—completely—how exhausting and tiresome and anxiety-rife the Trump era is, but maybe it's because we can afford to be.

Does any of this make sense to you?

It should. Could it be that in peacetime, violent discourse can be endured, and even enjoyed because it's untethered to real, measurable suffering? Politics is now filling space, but it's in a new form. It's *American Idol* all the time, and the loud, hilarious obnoxious judge is president, and none of us can stop thinking or talking about it. But the thing is, that antagonizing judge is pretty stingy with blood and treasure. He's not interested in spending our money abroad protecting people who should be protecting themselves, nor is he willing to send our kids to their deaths for the same damn thing. So there's that.

It's worth bringing up when anyone (including yourself) mentions the sheer emotional cost of having an anomalous president like Trump: that *I'll take a few sleepless hours in exchange for fewer bombs blowing up Americans.*

Let's return to the original premise: there's no break to

this intense conflict—it's a nonstop debate. There are only sixteen games in an NFL season, followed by playoffs and an off-season. And with baseball, spring training was initially designed to get flabby drunks back in shape for opening day after months of disrepair and debauch. With politics we don't need spring training—we need the opposite—the wind-down. We need what the Mets do every October.

I wrote a song about this with John Rich. It was called "Shut up about politics." It went to number one on the country charts, and for a few days was the highest-selling single in America. It made a lot of money—not for me, but for my second-favorite charity. Its popularity tells me that we could all use a break: we've been playing this game year-round.

A lot of it is fun, but we gotta dial it back. Initially it was great to "own the libs" every day, but sooner or later you're just owning yourself, because you're just being obnoxious for effect. In effect, you're emulating the worst aspects of your adversaries. It's great to fight back, but it's also great to keep the powder dry and pick your battles. (I say this, knowing that Trump picks every battle.) But if you treat this like a sport, then you need to introduce an off-season, a bye, a break—that forty-eight-hour span that allows your broken muscle tissue to rebuild. There are ways to do this, and they're painfully obvious, but we ignore them, because we're always in the middle of the game. And also, if you decide to take a break, that doesn't mean the other side does, too. If anything, they'll see your hibernation as an opportunity. You see the problem?

I'm not going to say, "Just go outside." I'm not going to say, "Read a book." Because you already are. But if you enjoy a good fight, taking a breather will make you that much better a fighter and breather. (My advice: Thrash metal.)

But what if others don't wish to take a break? What if they just can't stop? Then you need to learn how to direct traffic. Me? It's unavoidable that politics comes up because my job is 89.5 percent politics (I subtracted the stories we do on animals and fast food—which are often the same). But polarizing discussions can't be polarizing if only one pole shows up. And sometimes just a buttoned-up response to any hyper inquisitor is enough to make that angry pole seem very, very alone. The challenge, of course, is that Trump has replaced the weather as the topic for small talk just about anywhere. He is his own storm front, a number one content provider that beats every hurricane without even being winded. Every day, there's a 100 percent chance of Trump. My goal is always to turn any potentially negative-sounding conversation into a plus—and the best way is with one word: "So?"

I learned that from my dear pal the late Andrew Breitbart.

He used it on me when I brought up a concern about Donald Trump claiming that he wanted to host the debates (I think this was back in 2011). I had posed the question on my show *Red Eye*, expecting the usual dismissal of Trump that one heard daily from the media class. Not from AB. He just said, "So?" Which required me to actually follow through with my reasons for Trump not hosting the debates—and I had none. I wasn't expecting the "so."

But Andrew was ahead of the game on Trump. This is what he said in 2011 when it was noted that Trump was no conservative: "But this is a message to those candidates who are languishing at 2 percent and 3 percent within the Republican Party who are brand names in Washington, but the rest of the country don't know . . . celebrity is everything in this country. And if these guys don't learn how to play the media the way that Barack Obama played the media last election cycle and the way that Donald Trump is playing the election cycle, we're going to probably get a celebrity candidate." Okay, *How amazing is that quote?*

As this book barrels toward a close, it's fitting to bring up Trump, who seems to be everywhere at once. An analogy I often use: the clichéd horror movie in which the full cabin of victims frantically come up with idiotic solutions to protect against the impending maniac (Jason, Freddie Krueger, Meryl

Streep). That's what happens when a group of Never Trumpers get together.

It's why I didn't write a book about Trump. Everyone and their mother's personal trainer is doing one. And every one of those books becomes outdated as it hits the shelves, because Trump moves faster than the publishing world (which isn't hard). Plus the books are all the same, and can be split into two factions, or prisons, if you will. There are the anti-Trump books that focus all their intensity on what we already know is backstabbing gossip, his volatile personality, his abrasiveness, his "I don't give a fuckery." The other faction heralds a golden-haired god who changed politics forever.

My question: Why can't it be both? Because it is, really. I mean, couldn't Trump be the most obnoxious leader in modern history who drives some people mad, but also an actual and very necessary political phenomenon who's doing seriously great things?

Damn—I swore this book wasn't gonna be about Trump, but here I am writing about Trump! It's amazing how when you're running out of words, all you need to do is think of Trump, and that battery gets charged.

THE PLUS

"When you spend your lunch with me, you're
gonna end up more like me."

—Scott Adams, November 23, 2019

It sounds like a threat, and it is.

Adams said that in one of his Periscopes—which took place on one Saturday morning, and it may be the most powerful thing anyone has ever said about anything.

The highly successful, prolific cartoonist and unorthodox thinker was responding to some troll giving him shit for appearing to engage with someone considered by the media as "problematic." This is the new game in cancel culture: if we can tie you to someone who's a creep, then we can label you a creep, too—and ruin your life.

Understandably, this gruesome little trick pissed off Adams, as it pisses off everyone, including me. I still get tweets from losers who are always trying to implicate me by connection to other people. "In 2008 you had Clarence McGoogey on *Red Eye* and are you aware he's now running a horse brothel in Tampa!" If you happen to take a selfie with someone who later does something horrible, then you're 90 percent as guilty as that person.

Recently, Pitchfork, a music website, pursued veteran singer Thelma Houston for having the audacity to perform a duet on Morrissey's new album. Why? Because his beliefs have taken a hard right turn (despite his also being a hard-core vegan and animal rights activist). Rather than applaud the return of a great singer, and a novel collaboration—they chose to see this laudably creative adventure through their pathetic political eyes.

If you follow Adams's Periscopes, you know he rejects anyone telling him who he can be seen with, or who he can talk to.

And his quote above is all you need to say when anyone accuses you of hanging out with unsavory types, or people they deem "problematic." It's also the beginning of a philosophy one should adopt to counter the cancel culture.

Adams's theory is simple, and powerful.

If you sit down with someone who's a jerk, it's not like he's going to turn you into a jerk. If anything he will walk away from your meeting less of a jerk—simply by being around you.

It is hoped that whoever meets with you—no matter how despicable their beliefs are—will have *you rub off on them*, not the reverse.

Sorry, Scott, but there is something a little Christlike about it—Jesus did hang with the malcontents with the purpose of reforming them, even if it tarred his reputation.

There's something very brave about it—for it entails risk.

It's a selfless act to meet with, say, a racist, because no doubt you will be reviled for sitting with the reviled. But should you? What if, instead of urging public shaming and alienation, we saluted those like Adams (or Joe Rogan or Dave Rubin) who are willing to talk to anyone, as a method to shake someone of their hate?

Obviously, none of us are responsible for converting assholes, bigots, and abusers. In fact, it's probably a good thing to avoid them. But the idea that somehow crossing paths infects you, rather than the reverse, goes against the whole point of progress.

Progress is about moving forward, no? And shedding bad ideas, for better ones.

Breaking bread with the bad may be the only way to get the bad to see the light.

But what if I hate a person? The very worst thing I do: I think about it. I think about it a lot. Probably because hate is a good, rich feeling that allows you to deposit so much emotion into one parking space. It's exercise for your angst.

But on its heels comes a gross self-loathing—because you realize that this feeling is taking too much space in your head, and you're better than that. So you mentally kick yourself for thinking too much about this piece of trash, the person I hate, that piece of trash who wronged you. But still, you gotta stop thinking about it. But you don't.

Over time the hate fades, slowly. When it finally floats away, you will feel a weight has been lifted. Not because you think of this person in a better light, but because you don't think of them at all.

There are ways to reduce the hate. One of them is forgiveness—nothing new on that horizon. We can find it trite, but I think we all felt "something" when we saw that much-televised court scene in 2019 when a young man, Brandt Jean, forgave a female police officer for entering his brother's home and shooting his brother, Botham, dead. I realized if that guy could forgive the murderer of his brother, then surely I can forgive some douche bag who trashed me to my boss.

I also think about the opposite case: the people I have hurt. Did they forgive me?

Yes, I have pissed off people, and hopefully they've forgiven me. Perhaps because they realize that most harm in life is unintentional. That cop didn't intend to kill that man's brother: it was an accident. Most of our screwups are just that. Accidents. Hers was, however, the worst kind. And yet she was forgiven.

I've upset people in my life, unintentionally. And it took a lot for a few of these people to see that. I've forgiven people, and people have forgiven me. But the healthiest people I know don't ever think of these conflicts after the dust settles. How do you do that?

For me it's imagining the steps they took that brought them to doing the thing that hurt me.

Above all, was it intentional? If it wasn't, no matter how large the infraction is, it sucked but you almost always have to accept the apology. Even if that man ran over your dog, or that lady burned your house down—their stupidity, their drunkenness, their carelessness—it's repugnant. Deeply regrettable. But they probably know that. If they don't then they're sick. If they can't understand the ramifications of their actions, then the sooner you get away the better. Remember, the thing that killed Judas wasn't guilt. It was being sure he could never be forgiven.

My guess is that most people aren't aware how they hurt people, and the few that do are psychopaths. So it's pretty clear: forgive the first group if they ask for it, and run screaming from the second group. And try never to think of them again. In other words, forgive them by forgetting them. That's a plus.

WHY YOU MATTER

How's that for a chapter heading? How could you not read what follows? I mean, even if the next thousand words are garbage, you still gotta get to the end, with that promise. So I'm going to do my best to fulfill your expectations.

But to draw this out, I will start with how I figured out why *I* mattered. Trust me, this will end in a happy, positive note that will lift your spirits—or make you vomit. For me, it often happens at the same time.

It begins with music—mainly the music that I assign to bump in my segments on *The Five*. My musical choices reflect genuinely the stuff I listen to at home. It's a jarring mixed bag from '70s punk to '90s industrial, from 1960s surf to 1980s psychedelia. I play Turkish psyche, Australian shoegaze, Central American pop. The bands I pick are usually never ever played on what we once called "the radio." They include, regularly, The Cramps, Tobacco, Melvins, Mr. Bungle, Power Trip, Devin Townsend, Public Image, Mike Patton, Gang of Four, X, Wire, and even super-obscure stuff like SVT, Tuxedomoon, and Snakefinger. I can safely say that the majority of my colleagues on *The Five* find my music barely listenable. Once in a while, their ears might perk up to some melody, hook, or beat, but it's not interesting enough for them to write down the name of the band when I tell them who it is. I've had mild tiffs over this: "Why do you play stuff viewers never heard of?" Jesse asks me at least once a week.

My answer is "Because it's stuff viewers never heard of." You guys can play the popular stuff, the fan-favorite country hits, and I'll stick to the stuff they'd never hear were it not for me. And maybe they'll like it. (As it turns out, more than a few Fox viewers share my tastes, which says something terrifying about a few Fox viewers.)

But it's way more than that. I've asked myself why I curate tunes every day, when I can just leave it to the producers and instead focus on my hair like Jesse does his, but I realize it's not about music, it's about my role not on TV, but on earth.

When I was twenty, I was a funny little punk. I drank, I

fought, I listened to the Dead Kennedys, and hung out at tiny clubs and dingy record stores. But more and more I found myself put off by the reflexive liberalism of my peers, and more attracted to views that could be construed as conservative. I found myself laughing at the self-obsessed anger of the lefties on the Berkeley campus that I endured for four years, as I started reading right-leaning mags like *National Review* and *The American Spectator*. When I graduated from Cal, I ended up taking an internship in Washington, DC, at a conservative journalism outfit. There I stood out like a stocky sore thumb. I had little in common with many of my fellow interns, who were devoutly religious lifelong conservatives. They were good people, but many of them weren't my people.

So, when acquaintances who think they know me ask me in disbelief, "Greg, why in hell did you become a conservative?" I always say, "I didn't join conservatives to become a conservative. I joined conservatism so they would become me."

I realized that if someone like me couldn't stand the Left, and found the Right's ideas persuasive but still their whole world stodgy and close-minded, I had only one choice—not to join that new world but have that new world join me. And let me, platonically, of course, rub off on them. I had to infect the right with Gutfelditis. Yep, I needed them to be more like me—looser, weirder. They should be willing to laugh, be absurd, and risk offending people. They needed to stop taking themselves seriously. I was the one to help them do that, for sure. At the very least, I need to get them to wear less khaki.

So, now you see the point of the eclectic music choices—it's an effort to make some kind of headway into a world that could use some surprise, some oddity. I realize my role is that. To infect everyone around me with whatever I have (that isn't legitimately contagious). It's my way of reproducing without actually reproducing!

At one point, on *The Five*, Jesse looked at me and said, "Greg, you can't force everyone to be like you." He correctly identified my aims, but that wasn't going to stop me.

So that's my purpose in life . . . that's why I matter.

How does that help you? Well, because I believe that my purpose is also yours. You're here on this planet, so your good qualities rub off on other people. Every day you have the potential in front of you for leaving a mark on someone in both a good way and a bad way: the plus or the minus . . .

Which is the point of this book.

What you value about yourself—that plus—must be shared—if anything, to cancel out the negatives that are shared accidentally or deliberately by others. You are here on this planet to add your own positive attributes—your pluses—to the places that really need them. They need you more than you need them.

Joining a group, for example, isn't to make your life better. It's for you to make the others in that group better by absorbing the goodness in you. If you decide you want to join the Young Republicans, it shouldn't be because you want to be a Young Republican—it's that you want to make them better by knowing the cooler, funnier you. Likewise, if you're a liberal and want to join the Young Democrats, it's not simply to advance their cause but to bring what you have, as a forgiving person, to a group that could remember the art of forgiveness. The Right could always loosen up, but the Left needs to forgive more and cancel less. At this rate, there won't be any liberals left to cancel.

I've edited magazines, written books, helmed TV shows, and I've met most conservative leaders from the boldfaced names on down. And I'm the same freak I was when I was twenty. I hope that through these three decades of floating in and out of the shallow pools of pop culture that my lurid presence has had some positive impact. It must be a plus!!! And if it's not, then this book was a total waste.

Take *Red Eye*, which will remain the weirdest show, perhaps ever (with the possible exceptions of *Fernwood 2 Night* and Chris Elliot's brilliant *Get a Life*), and, yes, it was on Fox News! Despite having Fox News regulars on the show, it certainly didn't feel like Fox News. Instead it burned its own warped path, late at night even by a drug addict's standards, attracting people who never would have turned on the channel. They found *Red Eye* by accident, and were repulsed, confused, and then addicted.

That show was, for me, a strategy to impact conservatism by giving it an injection of manic, surreal absurdity. We had guests ranging from GWAR's late front man, Oderus Urangus, to John Bolton. We're probably the only show ever to be guest-hosted by Mike Huckabee, who also featured Johnny Rotten, King Buzzo from the Melvins, and other metal titans. I still think we're the only show to feature Black Moth Super Rainbow, and Ron Paul, while having the band Train write a song about us. Amy Schumer and Steven Crowder fought over the merits of virginity, other guests were often high, drunk, or both, and our pathetic staff once played softball against a team of strippers, where one table dancer chipped my tooth. But I am digressing into a dark hole.

Red Eye may be an obscure footnote in TV land, but I know it impacted the network, and you. Because of it, I ended up on *The Five*—and, yes, on that show, I cleaned myself up a little but not a lot. I still try to create chaos if the show gets too comfortable. I still say things that sound dirty but aren't—and, yes, I still play my godforsaken music.

In that way, I feel that I matter. It's like I am leaving a mark. And that's all you have to do in this world, is leave a mark. Just make it a plus, not a minus. You can be remembered for both, but only one, fondly.

ACKNOWLEDGMENTS

Special thanks to those who took part in this book: my editor, Natasha Simons; my hardworking manager, Aric Webb; my ultra-super-agent who never gets fat, Jay Mandel; and also all the folks I enlisted to read and add their thoughts, which include Denis Boyles, Paul Mauro, Joe Escalante, and Dana Perino. I also always appreciate the support of all the folks at Fox News from Suzanne Scott to the malcontents at *The Greg Gutfeld Show* (Tyrus, Kat Timpf, Tom O'Connor, Tom Shillue, Holly Cirelli, Gene Nelson, Joanne McNaughton, Gabby, and James). And of course there are all the freaks on *The Five*—including my long-suffering cohosts, Dana, Jesse, and Juan. Also thanks to the idiosyncratic thinkers who have influenced my brain, which include Scott Adams, Eric Weinstein, Dave Rubin, and Walter Kirn. And thanks to the artists whose music gets me through the writing—King Buzzo, Power Trip, and Devin Townsend, among others. Later!